Estate Agent's Secrets

The Hidden Secrets
The Top Performers In The Industry
Don't Want You To Know
(they work for letting agents too...)

Volume III - Execute

Silas J. Lees

ESTATE AGENT'S SECRETS

The Hidden Secrets The Top Performers In The Industry
Don't Want You To Know
(they work for letting agents too...)

Volume III - Execute

ISBN: 9798841489917

This publication is designed to provide accurate and authoritative information regarding the subject matter covered. It is sold with the understanding that the publisher is not engaged in rendering legal, accounting, or other professional services. If you require legal advice or other expert assistance, you should seek the services of a competent professional.

Disclaimer: The author makes no guarantees to the results you'll achieve by reading this book. All business requires risk and hard work. Your results may vary when undertaking any new business venture or marketing strategy.

DEDICATION

We dedicate the estate agent's secrets book series to all those people who are determined enough to make their dreams come true. Those of you who continually face uphill struggles, setbacks, and disappointments in life, yet keep on going no matter what.

The road to personal and business success is long and winding; full of learning opportunities which bring challenges and frustrations, yet those determined souls who keep digging deep and keep trying 'just one more time' know, that one day soon, it will all be worthwhile.

You are the true heroes in life and our source of inspiration. Thank you for being all that you are.

Welcome to the Property Revolution, we're just getting started.

DISCLAIMER

Unfortunately, in today's litigious society, we must state that the ideas shared within this book do not, in any way, constitute financial advice and we are not regulated by the FCA or any other financial or other professional regulated authority.

We're not qualified to make any such claims regarding the merits or otherwise of a particular investment, particularly within an economy that is greatly uncertain at the time of writing (March 2022).

We encourage all parties reading our books to seek sound and competent financial guidance from a suitably qualified professional in accordance with the law. We also encourage all parties to seek sound and competent legal guidance from suitably qualified lawyers.

The author and WiggyWam Limited, it's directors or employees cannot, and will not, be held responsible for any errors or omissions contained within this book and share the information contained within as ideas and suggestions only.

Finally, it's fair to say we're not professional writers, and there will be some small errors and omissions within the text. We ask that you take the substance of the book on board rather than getting caught up in the small detail that detracts from your learning.

CONTENTS

INTRODUCTION

THE FINAL SECRETS YOU'VE BEEN WAITING FOR...

Welcome to Volume III in the Estate Agent's Secrets Trilogy. We're thrilled you've made it this far on your journey with us and we know you'll have received a ton of value from the first two Volumes by successfully laying the foundations for building a hugely profitable company.

If you haven't gone through the first two Volumes yet, or you haven't done the exercises so far, we strongly encourage you to go back and do the hard yards before committing to this final book. Whilst it's tempting to get carried away with all the "sexy stuff," putting a proper foundation and automated nurture program into your business as we've outlined in Volumes I & II will ensure it stands the test of time for years to come.

You'll also receive at least 3x the reward for your efforts invested into Volumes I & II as you'll see by the end of this book. So, it makes sense to do the work and follow the roadmap we've laid out for you.

If you haven't got all three volumes, you can grab them here: http://www.wiggywam.co.uk/estateagentssecretstrilogy

And if you need any extra help, we're only a quick email away – HappyToHelp@WiggyWam.co.uk

Getting Stuck In

As a reminder, here's the promises we made at the start of Volume I, which we trust you'll hold us to as you work through this final Volume:

1) To deliver value far in excess of the purchase price (a minimum 10x return on your investment – think buying £1,000 note for only £100).
2) The opportunity to increase your fees to a level not seen before within your practice (and above that of your competition).
3) As well as raising your fees, we'll also show you how to win more instructions.
4) Reduce timescales for your property deals, so you get paid far more quickly and reduce the burden on your cashflow.
5) As a result of increased fees and reduced timescales for your deals, the natural consequence is increased profits in your business at the end of the trading year. As you'll discover later, this can automatically increase the value of your company by a factor of three!
6) With increased profits, you'll be able to afford better quality staff and better systems, so you'll enjoy working less hours on the coalface of the business and have more time to focus on the important work, (leaving you less stressed).
7) As a result of all of the above, your business should be well run, leaving you with peace of mind and enjoying more of the trappings of success.

These are significant promises to make and by now you'll have realised the content we've provided backs them up.

More importantly, we're given you the secret roadmap to help quickly improve the profits of your business. So do yourself a favour: commit to finishing this final book if you want the results you're searching for.

(Also, if you're at this final stage without an "Accountability Partner" we highly encourage you to get one as you follow this roadmap. If you have a trusted agency friend who you also think would benefit from the same goals, we encourage you to get them on board with your learning journey, so you have someone to bounce ideas off and get into the detail with.

Send them to: http://www.wiggywam.co.uk/estateagentssecretstrilogy and make a commitment to one another that you'll hold each other accountable to your promises of both finishing AND IMPLEMENTING the secret roadmap to agency success.

As we know life is busy and things get in the way, sometimes committing to finishing the task you've started can become a little overwhelming. So, if you're struggling to get an accountability partner, or just want someone to hold your hand through the transformation, we've created a fast-track 12-week accountability program to help you implement all these secrets into your business, so reach out to us if you think we can help – HappyToHelp@WiggyWam.co.uk)

Here's What's Required

No doubt you've tried to solve a lot of these problems on your own, or you've read some books by industry experts, or you've even gone on some webinars/seminars to learn from those people who tell you they know more than you. But there's one thing which no-one has shared with you, and that's the secret treasure map to help you find your way to the riches you desire.

Bad analogy? Not at all.

You see, we're willing to bet that trying to solve the biggest challenge in your business, is as frustrating as it is futile, and the reason for that is, it's not just one problem you need to solve, much to the dismay of all the "experts" out there telling you to solve one issue and all your dreams will come true. The harsh truth is, there's no point in trying to generate more leads for your business if your conversion rate to new instructions is pitifully low. There's no point trying to 'learn social media' when your business doesn't effectively deal with the gold mine of opportunity its currently sitting on.

What you need, which these series of books are all about, is presenting this secret roadmap which takes you through a nine-step process to get you from Point A to Point B, and which leaves no stone unturned in your pursuit of excellence. And if you're already feeling overwhelmed at what could be a huge task, don't worry as we've got you covered. We've done as much of the work as possible to give you all the tools, knowledge, and information necessary to transform your business from run-of-the-mill, to the best agency in town.

The only thing required from you at this stage is to just commit to the process and trust that what we're taking you through will be to your ultimate benefit.

Suspend your ego and turn down the volume on the negative voice in your head that says, "I already know this" because – as the old saying goes - 'To know, and not to do, is not yet to know.'

We trust you'll set aside the idea of indulging in mental masturbation to intellectually understand this information, and instead, get your hands dirty as you embrace a new way of doing things that will make a huge difference to your business.

Now if all this seems a little too much, take inspiration from the face that your competition will still be doing what everyone else is doing and most likely won't bother picking up this book or exploring the information further through our other training, resources, or learning centre. Besides which, literally nobody else in the industry is teaching this depth of information, so you're already ahead of like 95% of other agents out there.

And for that, we salute you! But don't rest on your laurels – Take ACTION!

As the saying goes, 'ideas are a dime a dozen, its effective execution that makes them valuable'. We couldn't agree more, so let's get cracking on this exciting journey together.

Finally, we were going to make this offer at the back of each book as a reward for those readers who took the time to seek out all the key learnings and implement them in their business. However, realising how busy we all are, and the uphill struggle we're all going to be faced with as we head out of the pandemic, (into potentially World War Three and as out-of-control inflation begins to bite), we wanted to try and help as many people as possible put these learnings into practice in their business.

So, as a reward for simply buying this book, and for being the forward-thinking agent you are, we'd like to offer you exclusive access to a highly effective training course which will literally take you by the hand and walk you through each of the ideas presented here to help you rapidly implement them within your business.

The key focus of the training is to:

1. Help you win more instructions
2. Help you increase your fees

3. To flood your pipeline with more (profitable), work than you can handle
4. Reduce your stress and workload

This exclusive closed-door training is valued at over £5,000 and we have limited seats available to service the high level of demand we're experiencing as a result of publishing this book series.

To be honest with you, this is not your average training and requires us to dedicate a huge amount of personal time and resources to support agents in their journey to become the best agent in their area, so don't know how long we'll be able to make this available for, or how many people we can realistically accommodate (it won't be many).

So, if you'd like to grab one of the last remaining seats, simply email us: HappyToHelp@WiggyWam.co.uk with the heading; "Make me a VIP" and send us a screenshot of your purchase for the opportunity to get on board whilst it's still available.

Helping Others

Once you've received value from this book, we'd really appreciate you recommending it to a fellow agent, friend, or relative in the industry who can also take the opportunity to grow and expand their business. We trust they'll find much greater value in the secrets shared than the cost of this book.

BUT, if you truly want to help them, **don't** give them this book for free…

Here's why…

For some bizarre reason, humans will take action to hoard a precious resource, but won't necessarily take action to use that resource, especially if they had to exert little effort to obtain it. Think about how many times you've grabbed free stuff off the internet and never read it because it wasn't a high enough priority to read it during your busy day.

So, if you give this away for free, the odds are against your friend ever using it. We didn't design human psychology, it's just the way it is – if you truly want to help them, get them to buy the book by sending them to http://www.wiggywam.co.uk/estateagentssecretstrilogy

Also, if you like the idea of being rewarded and learning more, please find the time to leave an honest review on Amazon, to not only inspire other people, but to give us the opportunity to bring more learnings, knowledge and wisdom to you in future editions. Your clients, your industry, and you yourself deserve the best, so thank you for striving to be the best of the best.

Finally, if you have any suggestions on how we can improve these books, or to share lessons learnt or helpful stories to assist others, please get in touch via: HappyToHelp@WiggyWam.co.uk

We look forward to working with you very soon,

Silas and all the team at WiggyWam.

Welcome to the Property Revolution, we're just getting started.

CHAPTER ONE

SECRETS OF CLIENT RETENTION

A Quick Check-In

If you've done the work, we trust you've been able to uncover some absolute gems that have not only helped you identify a bunch of problems your clients are facing, but also how you can bring solutions to the table to help them, and profit from it at the same time.

After all, isn't that just what business is all about? Finding problems that need to be addressed, providing the market with a solution, and then letting the market decide exactly how valuable that service is?

As entrepreneurs and business owners, there's always the temptation to look at all the new, exciting, and shiny stuff rather than simply knuckling down and grinding out the mundane and everyday stuff, even though that's your 'bread and butter' which helps keep the lights on. That's why we've saved this Volume until last, and if you've had the patience to work through all the ideas we've presented in Volumes I & II, and taken action to implement them, then you'll have put the foundations in place for a truly solid business.

The alternative is to start with all the hot, new stuff, not fix the current problems in your business, and find the whole thing topples over when you start bringing in more business than you and your team can realistically handle. And we don't know about you, but that doesn't sound like a winning strategy!

So, do yourself a favour, get the right foundations in place, even if it takes you a year to do it before you start trying to amplify your results by implementing this Volume. Otherwise, you could end up losing not just your business, but your reputation if you start trying to do more, but you can't deliver on your promises.

As ever though, you're all adults so you will make up your own minds as to what to do. So, without any more lecturing, onwards and upwards!

Client Retention

In line with getting distracted by all the new stuff, let's have a look at something which most businesses, including (especially?!) the 'big boys' get wrong all the time. And that's client or customer retention. And let's kick off by asking you this key question:

How big would your business truly be if you retained <u>every single client</u> you served?

We're not talking about every client you did a valuation for, but who instructed you to sell or let their property, and you followed it through to the completion of the deal. And not only that, but those clients also came back to you every time they had a property to sell or let, whether that be an investment, another home, or selling a property for a deceased estate?

If you pause to think about it for more than a minute or two, chances are the diamonds under your feet are beginning to make themselves visible. Yet how many companies not only do a horrible job of client retention, but go one step further to alienate past and present clients from their business <u>by offering all the new customers the best deals…?</u>

How many times have you seen TV ads directed at "new customers only"? You've more than likely noticed them when you're a customer of that particular business and you realise you're getting fleeced, whilst someone with no track record, no customer loyalty, and no trading history with the firm is getting a much better deal. Mobile phone companies are probably the worst, as are internet providers, and virtually any other business that relies on subscription services (stop it – we know who you're thinking about and we never mentioned them…ok?!).

And how does it make you feel? Taken advantage of? Disappointed? Even angry...?

You're not alone. Shouldn't it be the other way around? That you're rewarded for customer loyalty? And if so, what should they be doing to not just win you as a new customer, but to retain you for the long term?

Some agents might push back and argue that a client only sells a property once every 7-10 years, so it's almost impossible to breed loyalty. And on the surface, that sounds like a logical argument. So, let's look at it in the cold light of day.

When you sell a property for a client, they pay you a commission. That much is obvious. And the average commission across the country is around £3,174.00 (based on average house price of £256,000 (March 2022) and average commission percentage of 1.24%). Now, that might not seem like a lot to you, but to your client, you can bet they will have had at least one discussion about 'The King's Ransom' they've had to pay the agent who sold their home. And if you're particularly unlucky, they will have had that discussion with a less than favourable tone with friends over drinks or at a dinner party. And those types of conversations tend to stick in the minds of most people, especially if they live in the same area and they're thinking about moving home sometime soon...

Now, regardless of how unfair you feel that viewpoint is, the client gave you their business and after it was done, they might have received a thank you card and maybe a bottle of wine or flowers, but what then? For most agents, its likely they'll have failed to keep in contact with their past client, other than perhaps seeing them around town once in a while.

Fast forward seven years later now they need to move again, and they're thinking about who to use. They could use you again, but there's that lingering feeling that you could have 'done better', so they decide to explore options with other agents. And when push comes to shove, it's likely they'll go with someone else.

Why?

Well because they already know what to expect, and "maybe" someone else will be a bit different? Unfair? Maybe, but ask yourself, could you have kept in contact with them, if you really wanted to?

"But Silas! Keeping in contact with a past client will cost us a fortune! We couldn't afford to do it!"

Ok. Relax. Standard answer, but is there any truth in it? How much does it cost to email someone, really? Its practically free. And to send a Christmas card once a year? Maybe £1-2. So, the total cost so far is about £14 plus a bit of time to make this happen.

(The Christmas card is particularly useful because when do most people think about moving home? During the holidays when the family are all together (or when they've finally had two weeks together and realise they hate one another and want to split up)).

So, let's ask this question:

"Would you pay £14 for a red-hot lead if you knew they were going to instruct you to sell their property (again)?"

It's a total no-brainer, isn't it?

Even if you wanted to get a bit fancy and do some extended outreach to past clients, you're talking about investing a little behind the scenes time to structure your client nurturing program and then it's in place pretty much forever. Let's push the boat out. Let's say it costs you £200 over 10 years in outreach costs to win back a past client. Still worth it?

£20 a year to win at least the average fee of £3,174 (with virtually no competition), next time they decide to sell. Is this a good investment of your marketing budget? Or should you keep shooting blind at your target and rely on chance to win new business in the future?

More importantly, do you think if you've kept in contact with a past client for 7-10 years, and provided useful value to them, they'll automatically think you're worth more in comparison to your competition? Hopefully you agree the answer is an automatic yes, and you'll also see this as a fantastic excuse to increase your fees (not just to cover the cost of marketing to past clients).

Network, Network, Network

If you're excited by this idea, let's take it a step further and look at something even more powerful. We've all heard of the power of networking and how its crucial if you want to grow your business. But how do you do this efficiently in estate or letting agency?

We believe the most time efficient way of doing this is to get your clients to do it for you. And why would they do this? Because you're going to offer them an incentive to do so.

Think about how powerful a referral is. You've more than likely received one from a friend or family member in the past. Someone said to you, "Oh, you just <u>have</u> to read this book" and you bought it without hesitation. Or they told you about a movie or a place to eat, and you went along willingly because the recommendation came from a trusted source.

So why should it be any different when someone comes to choose the right agent to work for them? Key point, it doesn't have to be. And if you're providing exceptional value, all the way through this process, and keeping in touch well after the deal has completed, guess who is going to be singing your praises when it comes up in conversation (verbally or online)?

You've guessed it – your very grateful past clients!

And is there a way to incentivise people to do business with you? What about a referral fee? Do you think someone would be motivated to point their friends and family in your direction if you were offering a Fortnum & Mason hamper, or £200 worth of M&S vouchers for their efforts? Not incentive enough? How about £300? £400? £1,000?

And before you say it's not profitable, remember this phrase as you go throughout this book:

"The Deal Pays"

It doesn't matter what amount you pay as a referral fee, as long as the deal pays for itself. If you expect to make £2,500 commission, could you afford to give away £250 to someone who brings the business to you? And rather than front-load your costs, could you split the fee by doing £50 up front and the balance on completion? Or any other variable of these numbers?

Getting creative with this is how you drive more value into your business and the reason we've started with these examples is because you're going to see how powerful they become as the rest of this book unfolds.

So, buckle up and jot down all the ideas that come into your mind as you're reading, because they have the power to make you a fortune.

Working Together

As a slight Segway from referrals and retentions, is the focus on making more money, particularly during the current stock shortages agents are experiencing in the market at the moment. As stock levels dry up, it puts more of a burden on cashflow – not immediately, but in 90-120 days' time as your pipeline begins to complete and there's been less deals entering the front end to replenish those you've been paid on.

So, one of the key working practices we think all agents should embrace right now is working together via the MLS service. This will also become more crucial as the market begins to cool and fall into the inevitable recession which is on the horizon. More stock will naturally become available, but it will get harder and harder for agents to find buyers, so working together is going to be vital to help them all stay in business.

The same thing happened not that long ago in 2008 where agents were literally trying to grab as much work as possible just to keep the lights on. One agent we know kept his business afloat only by doing EPC's as he couldn't sell anything once the credit crunch began to bite.

How Does The MLS Work And Why Should You Embrace It?

In short, it's very similar to doing a Joint Agency with another agent in your area, but in this case, you're making your stock list available to multiple agents in the hope that if another agent finds a buyer, you'll split your commission with them.

Whilst its natural to want to keep 100% of the pie to yourself, it's possible that doing so will force you out of business if you're struggling to get sales. That might seem impossible based on the last two years, but anyone who has been in agency for more than 20 years will tell you that the market can change quickly and get very tough indeed.

Besides, there's potential for you to make some serious cash with this strategy if you find partners to work with who are not a 'threat' to your business. Sometimes agents won't trust their local competitors enough to do MLS deals with them, but will trust an agent 200 miles away, because they're far enough away, in the agents mind at least, not to cause a problem!

When we move onto later sections in this book, you'll see why this could be such a great strategy to employ if you're serious about skyrocketing your revenue and making more money. Just keep this at the back of your mind for the time being and you'll see how all the pieces of the jigsaw fit together.

We promise we won't let you down!

Becoming The Go-To Expert In Your Area

To win more business and keep clients coming back to you, there's nothing better than becoming the go-to expert in your area. But the question is, how?

We've already explored a couple of different strategies in earlier Volumes which are helpful to guide you. The main one is building out your customer nurturing journey and getting it up and running so it not only attracts new clients, but also serves those who are currently, and were previously, working with you.

The simple point is this; the more you demonstrate your knowledge and expertise in a way that's visible, logical, and the client can access it (at least initially) without cost, or more importantly, without risk, the better you'll do. This is how people build up a huge following online, because they're giving away knowledge or information for free, or at low cost, which minimises the risk for the consumer. If you watch a YouTube video and you didn't like it much or didn't 'vibe' with the presenter, no harm done. You haven't been exposed to a big financial loss, so people move on.

But, if you loved what that person had to say, and they also gave you a free report, or a free consultation call, or other item of value (in exchange for your email address), the likelihood is, you're drawn to at least carrying out that exchange and taking the next step together. You might even be tempted to look them up on Amazon and buy their book if you found what they were saying to be useful. And once you bought their book and got value from it, you might be tempted to invest more in coaching or an online program they offered.

So, let's take a look at how we can build our authority with a free guide that offers some major value to lawyers…can you see where we're going with this… ;-)

If you want to see how you can really add value to your clients and your business, there's a ton of extra resources we can share with you on a call.

We just ask you to invest 30 minutes into a complimentary consultation, where we can help fast-track your success (with no hard sell whatsoever).

Here's the link to book your call:

http://www.wiggywam.co.uk/estateagentssecretscall

CHAPTER TWO

SECRETS TO BUILDING YOUR CLIENT NURTURING JOURNEY

It's one thing to talk about a client nurturing journey, and leave people to their own devices to decide what to do. It's another thing to give them an example which they can use which gives them some structure and format to help build their content offering for their target market.

Here's an example of the kind of value we offer our lawyer clients in the form of a lead magnet. As you're reading this, take special note of any elements which cause you to feel emotion, what that emotion is, and what triggered it within the text. Also, look at any actions you may feel like taking as a result of reading it.

Let's dive in…

WARNING: Do Not Attempt To Buy (Or Sell) Another Property For Your Clients Without Reading This Shocking Free Report…

Shocking report reveals the 5 things you must know about helping your clients move home that could cost them £thousands and threaten their livelihood.

For your clients, moving home conjures up beautiful images of them living in their perfect new space, enjoying lazy summer days in the garden listening to the sounds of birds tweeting as they enjoy good times with friends over a BBQ. And best of all, as a solicitor, you help your clients make their dreams come true.

BUT...

Moving home is the third most stressful thing a person can do, and it's not an exaggeration to say that your clients could end up seriously out of pocket or even in hospital if it all goes wrong!

This shocking report reveals behind-the-scenes secrets which we can say with confidence you won't find anywhere else. Information which can only be gained through blood, sweat, tears, and a lifetime spent in the property industry. Information that would literally cost you tens, if not hundreds of thousands to learn and which most people never get exposed to. And by not knowing the in-depth secrets I'm about to share in this shocking report, you could, like so many others, unwittingly put your law firm at risk of financial ruin.

Before we start, I should tell you that I've had the privilege of helping literally thousands of people navigate the hurdles, pitfalls and financial bear-traps that can rear their ugly head as they take steps towards buying (or selling) property.

With your permission, I'd like to offer to be your guide on navigating this difficult journey and share with you the hard-hitting facts on problems your clients will face along the way, and more importantly, how you can take direct steps to stop the main problems from happening which cripple so many people.

Without boasting, I'd like to reassure you that I've worked with some of the biggest names in the property industry, including Robbie Fowler (the footballer, who most don't know is a massive property investor), Martin Roberts (from the TV show Homes Under The Hammer), and Robert Kiyosaki (international best-selling author) which I hope gives you confidence in what I am about to share with you. I've also been a property investor for around 20 years, an estate agent, landlord and I'm a qualified Building Surveyor. I share this not to boast, but to give you an idea of the depth of my experience in the property world.

To keep this report as concise as possible, I'm going to leave out any fluff and give you the hard-hitting facts, even if it causes you to feel uncomfortable, stressed-out, or downright confused about the whole process. Don't worry though, because at the end of this guide, I'm going to show you how to stack the odds in your favour to make your clients' moving journey as effortless as possible and to help you, as solicitors, make your lives far easier and more profitable, simply by helping them achieve their goals.

So, let's dive straight in…

5 Simple Yet Powerful Tips
You Can Use To Help Your Clients Move Home Quickly
Without The Whole Process Killing You (Or Them)
– Even If You Don't Know Where To Start

Moving into your dream home is one of the greatest feelings someone can experience. There is simply nothing else like it. That's because when someone finally gets the keys to their new home, they can enjoy peace and tranquillity in the safety of their new surroundings, enjoy the feeling of being a homeowner, and finally live in the area they've wanted to be in for some time.

However, there are many obstacles your clients must overcome before they can get there. Not only do they have to deal with mortgage providers, surveyors, and estate agents, – but they also have to find a decent solicitor who can make the deal legally binding. This can be the most difficult challenge of all. Potential obstacles at each stage of the process can leave your client falling well short of the mark and prevent them from ever actually moving home and yet it could also leave them with a big legal bill to pay if it all goes wrong.

Fortunately though, moving home doesn't have to be as challenging for your clients as they may think. Far from it, in fact. Simply by implementing the right tried-and-tested techniques, you can help your clients buy or sell their dream home without experiencing any of the common frustrations.

How would we know?

Because, at WiggyWam we're experts at helping people move home in the shortest possible timeframe. Over the past 25+ years, we've helped hundreds if not thousands of clients finally achieve their desire of buying or selling properties without the endless weeks or months of hard work and trial and error most people usually have to endure.

We've written this eBook to share some of the most powerful secrets we've accumulated during our time in the property industry. The information you're about to read will help you speed up housing transactions and make more money whilst making sure you avoid months of frustration dealing with a process which has become progressively worse over the last few decades.

In fact, since the late 1990's, (and despite all the technology that we currently enjoy), the timescale for getting an offer accepted on a property to exchange of contracts has jumped from 6-8 weeks, to nearly 26 weeks today! And in some parts of the country, I am told its over 500 days!! Imagine banging your head against a wall for three times as long…that's the moving home process for people who don't have access to this expert knowledge and information.

You're about to discover:

- 5 simple tips you can use to help your clients move home quickly – even if you have no or little experience and don't know where to start.

- How to help your clients avoid the 3 most common mistakes made by home buyers and sellers – making even 1 of these errors could cost them thousands of pounds and set them back months in the process.

- 3 insider secrets that can help slash the moving time by as much as 70%, (much to the surprise of solicitors and estate agents) – number 2 will completely blow your mind!

- The TRUTH about the property industry's dirty little secrets that they don't want you to know and why most home buyers and sellers lose thousands or spend many frustrating months banging their head up against the wall trying to get the deal done.

By the time you've finished reading, you'll have all the information you need to kickstart your journey to success and help your clients move home without the headaches and frustration that most experience who don't have access to this information, (whilst adding more profit to your bottom line for working less hours)!

Be warned though, what I'm about to share with you may make you frustrated, even angry, at the state of the property industry and the hurdles that stop clients from reaching their goal. Together though, we'll get through them.

Let's get started!

5 Simple Yet Powerful Tips You Can Use To Help Your Clients Move Home Quickly

Some days, your client's vision of holding the keys to their dream home in their hand might seem like an impossible mission. But, if you help them implement the right strategies, they can get there far sooner than you think, whilst making the whole process more profitable and less stressful for you. We've outlined 5 simple, tried-and-tested techniques you can use to fast track your clients to rapidly buying or selling their home without the endless delays, stress, and frustration that most encounter by ignoring this process.

#1 Access To Up-Front Information

If you're serious about helping clients move home quickly, one of the first things you absolutely must do is to get access to as much up-front information as possible. It's vitally important your clients prepare their 'sellers pack' (a full pack of information relating to the property they're selling). This packs needs to be compiled before the client puts the property on the open market. If you're acting for a buyer, reviewing the sellers pack at the start of the deal can raise any red flags early on saving them hundreds, if not thousands of pounds in costs.

For example:

- In my property investing career, I bought lots of property at auction. Why? The simplicity of the process. The 'auction pack' contains most of the information needed to make an informed decision about the property and it gives everything the solicitors need to get the deal done very quickly. When a property goes to auction, the auctioneers spend 2-4 weeks collecting all the necessary information to form the auction pack which speeds up the transaction to the point where exchange of contracts happens on the day of the auction, and completion happens 7-28 days later. No frustrating delays and no headaches, as long as you've prepared properly.

- With a private treaty sale as opposed to an auction sale, the biggest problem which causes all the delays and frustrations in the moving process, is the lack of access to all the information required about the property. Solicitors are naturally cautious and want to make sure they aren't missing anything, so they'll go over all documentation like a forensics expert at a murder scene! If there's some vital piece of information missing, or they have questions, this slows the process down whilst they raise an enquiry, and someone has to find the piece of paper or provide an explanation for the situation. Solicitors who convey properties every day are immune to the frustrating back-and-forth delays and unfortunately aren't proactive enough in trying to reduce the time wasted on deals. Furthermore, they instinctively think they must raise an invoice for any work they do on behalf of a client. This mindset naturally makes clients nervous about working with them early on in the process.

- Solicitors are busy, and it's not uncommon for you to be working on 40, 60 or even 100 other cases at any one time. The constant starting-and-stopping process on each case drains a ton of time in each deal, as you need to pick each file back-up, refresh your memory, review any new information received and then raise further enquiries if you're not satisfied. Each new enquiry can literally take weeks to respond to, so can you see why it's so important to have access to all the information up front? I have literally sat in solicitor's offices where the floor was littered with piles and piles of brown folders; all relating to some poor client's property deal that was progressing very, very slowly. I'm sure this doesn't happen in your office, (mainly because most files are now digitised in case management software), however remember that out of sight equals out of mind, and because of the pressures of the job, most solicitors act in a way where the 'noisiest wheel gets the grease'.

- What most solicitors don't tell their clients is that you're underpaid and whilst you're good at what you do, you've never been taught how to run a business. As you weren't taught business at law school, most solicitors think the way to win work is to compete on price and price alone. After all, how do you sell a service? And aren't all solicitors and their service levels practically the same? This is a huge mistake! Whilst your client might think it's great that they can get their conveyancing done for £400, I can tell you from experience, it's a huge mistake to sell your service at this price.

- What happens behind the scenes is the solicitor isn't making much money on each case when they charge low fees, but they need to make more money to survive. So, what do they do? Try to take on more work! This leaves them swamped with low-profit work which increases their stress levels as they try and make ends meet! Who suffers the most? The client! Why? Because the solicitor literally cannot cope with all the cases they're working on at the same time. And we all know what constant high levels of stress can lead to – mistakes, delays, time off work, lack of a pro-active attitude or even alcoholism… This results in delays and frustration for all involved and turns what should be a simple 6-week process into 26+ weeks. Even worse, when clients or agents chase solicitors for a progress update, they look at the file, and realising nothing's happened for two weeks, they quickly rattle off a letter to the other side just so they can say they've taken some action, and put the file back down, magically hoping the conveyancing fairies will appear during the night to get the deal over the line! Of course, solicitors won't tell their clients this. We heartily recommend our clients steer clear of low-fee solicitor at all costs. Worst still, even if you are a highly efficient conveyancing operation, invariably you and your clients suffer significant delays when involved in a chain with solicitors who couldn't care less about their clients or their business (yes, there's more of these than you might think).

Getting early access to information helps solicitors deal with the majority of enquiries at the start of the deal and prevents the unnecessary back-and-forth process most buyers, sellers, solicitors, and estate agents frustratingly endure as they simply don't know any different.

At WiggyWam, we recommend sellers complete one of our easy-to-use online 'sellers packs' to gather the necessary information together at the start of the process to help move the deal along far more quickly. It might seem like a minor inconvenience for them to spend time gathering the information required now, but it has to be done eventually anyway, so they may as well do it right at the start and enjoy a relatively stress-free moving experience, rather than leaving it all to chance and running the risk of enduring months of frustration, losing their buyer, or losing their dream home as the whole process has taken far too long, but they still end up with a big legal bill for the pleasure.

#2 Charge Higher Fees

As well as getting access to as much up-front information as possible, you also need to be charging your clients higher fees if you're ever going to effectively help them buy or sell their dream home. We touched on this earlier, and whilst it may seem contrary to most solicitor's beliefs, this strategy is powerful because it can help your clients achieve their desired outcome in a MUCH shorter timeframe.

Most people don't realise the power a solicitor has in determining the outcome of a home buying or selling journey. The British public has a generally biased view against conveyancing solicitors, in the most part deeming them to be untrustworthy, slow, and an unavoidable inconvenience.

Having worked in the industry pretty much all my life, I can tell you that reputation is not exactly unfair. I've witnessed first-hand some absolutely shocking behaviour from solicitors and it's this not-knowing that puts a lot of people at risk.

I could share some real horror stories of encounters with rouge solicitors. Here's just a few examples that stick in the mind:

- When I was an estate agent chasing progress updates from one particular solicitor, she aggressively spat; "I'll get to that file when I am good and ready!" I bet the client was thrilled to have such a lazy lawyer acting for them!

- Solicitors who frequently quote a low fee for the legal work, then add a ton of other expenses on top of the fee quoted making them very expensive when compared to other solicitors.

- A local solicitor who couldn't cope with the volume of work he'd taken on and unfortunately succumbed to alcoholism; making a ton of mistakes on behalf of his clients before eventually getting suspended. What happened to his poor clients? A locum had to pick up where he'd left off and spent many months trying to rectify his drunken errors.

- The solicitor who actually sold his client's property to another buyer without telling anyone until he'd exchanged contracts on the other sale!

- Solicitors who frequently take fees for work they do not do. Yes, it's against regulations but it happens more frequently than the industry wants to admit.

- A rogue solicitor who bought tiny parcels of garden land in front of rows of terraced houses for a pittance, and then held the homeowners to ransom by demanding over £20,000 from each party to buy the land back, just so they could access their own houses!

- The many law firms I've seen that have claims against them from homeowners who found defects in the legal title as the law firm hadn't done a thorough enough job when they bought it. Are cheap fees really worth the potential liability?

So, with this background, why should solicitors charge their clients more? After all, surely everyone wants their deal done for the cheapest price possible? Not at all. What people want is:

- **Handholding through the deal** – they haven't moved home in years and solicitors have an annoying habit of assuming everyone knows what they do for their money. I'll let you in on a little secret; most, if not the overwhelming majority of home buyers and sellers (and plenty of estate agents), have no clue what a conveyancing solicitor does for their money. And perversely, the legal profession seems to prefer it this way, under the mistaken belief that the 'smoke-and-mirrors-air-of-superiority' around what they do somehow assists them. Well, I'm sorry to say that it doesn't, particularly when the younger generation are fully equipped with the use of technology and can track down answers to their questions in seconds online. Hold your client's hand through the deal and charge them for it accordingly. Not only will they thank you, you'll earn more too.

- **Education** – as touched on above, most clients don't know what you do during the conveyancing process or why. This lack of knowledge causes a ton of frustration for your clients when they're faced with deathly silence, a lack of communication, and they don't understand what needs to happen to get the deal across the line.

- **Pro-active service** – your prospective clients are totally and utterly fed up with solicitors who don't respond to their calls and emails. They're fed up with having to chase for a progress update (driven more by lack of education and fear of the unknown than anything else), and the deathly silence causes all parties to get annoyed as they think they're being ignored or are too far down the list of priorities for their solicitor to be bothered with. In a world of instant communication, your client, the one who is ultimately paying your fee, finds this completely unacceptable. And so they should.

- **Speed and efficiency** – everyone wants their transaction treated as a priority. I happen to know property investors who will willingly pay £2,000, £3,500, or even £5,000 for a basic conveyance, but they want the job done yesterday. They constantly complain that they cannot find reliable solicitors to work with on a regular basis. Here's a golden opportunity solicitors are missing out on, to massively increase the profitability of their business if only they'd stop fire-fighting for a few minutes to observe what's really going on in the market.

- **An innovate approach to problem solving:** This isn't what most people think, so I want to use an example to illustrate. Some time ago, I met with the owner of a large conveyancing firm to discuss the possibility of buying it. Despite the fact this guy was losing a fortune, he's still working in the business now and nothing has changed over the last 18 months. Anyway, during the conversation, he mentioned how frustrated he was with the time it was taking to get searches back and he'd been waiting over 8 weeks on this one particular deal. I enquired why he hadn't put search indemnity insurance in place to get the deal across the line immediately for his client. For a nominal cost, the deal would have been done. The blank stare I received back from him told me everything I needed to know. 40+ years in the conveyancing industry and it hadn't even crossed his mind to do this one little thing to help his client's out! For less than £100, he could have solved the problem almost instantly, and the client would have been all the happier because of it. Never forget, that until the deal is legally exchanged, either party can pull out at any moment, and that places your client directly at risk of losing their buyer, or losing the home of their dreams, or both. Sadly, the client, the one who's paying everyone's fees, is the one who's left out of pocket when things go wrong.

Only 8% Of Sellers Are Cost-Conscious

In a recent survey WiggyWam conducted with the home buying and selling public, we were shocked to discover that only 8% of people were cost-conscious when it comes to moving home. This is contrary to what we always 'knew'; people were cost-sensitive and wanted to scrimp and save as many pennies along the way as possible because moving home is not a cheap operation.

Wrong!

What was most revealing was the fact that they were prepared to pay more for services which made their moving experience smoother and hassle-free. And most importantly of all, that educated them about the processes involved.

How could you use that knowledge and information in your business? And how could you increase your service offering and fees accordingly? Take some time to reflect on these questions now and write some ideas down. They could be instrumental in creating a massive USP between you and your competition.

For more information, visit our learning centre at: www.wiggywam.co.uk/learn

#3 Offer More Perceived Value

One of the biggest frustrations ever shared by solicitors is that the general public won't pay higher fees, and as their competitors are all charging less, they have to reduce their own fees in order to win business.

The problem is simply that you're not showing your potential clients enough perceived value to justify a higher fee. I want you to focus on the words 'perceived value' in that sentence as you read it again.

The perception of value is subjective, depending upon the individual. Think about what is arguably one of the greatest symbols of wealth in the world; a Rolls-Royce. Now to some people, such a car represents significant value. The high quality of the materials. The design and engineering that's gone into it. The fact that its hand-built. The exclusivity of driving a world-renown marque that few can afford.

And for those people, the price tag is a bargain.

But if you look at a Rolls-Royce and compare it to say, a Ford Focus, and you're comparing the fact that they both have four wheels, both get you from A to B and both keep the wind and rain out, you're going to have a very hard time justifying the extra spend on buying a Roller.

They're both a vehicle, but there's two totally different perceptions of value.

So, what does this have to do with conveyancing fees? Well- think about the service that you're offering and how it stacks up against the competition. How does your service compare to the perceived market leaders locally, or across the country? Are you offering more perceived value than they are, or are you undercutting them on fees because you don't feel you can compete head-to-head? Or worse, is your whole pricing structure built around the idea that if a competitor is charging £700 +VAT, you should be able to win the business by charging only £650 +VAT, (whilst failing to take into account the actual time, effort and expertise required to do a thorough job for your client)?

So, the real question is, where are you underselling yourself and your services?

A Dose Of Reality

I can hear you saying; "Yes Silas, I already know this! Tell me something I don't know!" Well consider this; the majority of your competition are all operating in the same way. Taking the enquiry from the client, asking them a few questions about the property before telling them the fee and crossing their fingers in the hope they win the business. And out of every 3 lawyers that a potential client calls, you've got about a 33% chance of being selected as the winner, all things being equal.

Let's take this a step further. Detach yourself from your current position and put yourself in your client's shoes for a moment to think about what grounds a potential client has to distinguish between one law firm and another. It's harder than you think to do this exercise. It will pay you to draw up a comparison chart between you and your competition and look at each individual distinguishing point to see how you <u>really</u> differ from them. Is it the quality of your advertising (assuming you're doing any)? Is it your funky new website? Is it the fact that you use more experienced conveyancers in the process? Or is it the fact that your company has completed the most transactions in your local area?

If you're honest with yourself and can really step back from your position as a solicitor competing against your competition you'll see that in reality, your potential prospect, (who is not in your industry and who doesn't understand the true difference between one lawyer and another), they can only form an opinion on a very short customer journey, which is essentially a 5 minute telephone call and the follow up email they may receive (if they're lucky). That's pretty much it. They may check out your website and perhaps your press advertising, maybe even your office window if you're on the High Street, but you're leaving a lot to chance as far as winning their business is concerned.

And if you think about the other ways in which solicitors win business, they usually rely on recommendations because 'a client used their firm in the past', or because the solicitor has a referral system in place with local agents, who they end up paying most of their fee to in the form of a commission payment, further reducing the amount of money they make whilst putting excess pressure on all involved to try and make a profit.

The Most Overlooked Secret In The Legal World

A bold statement, I realise, however let's look at why selling your services to your potential clients seems to be so hard. And it's this:

What you're selling isn't tangible.

Your potential client can't really touch it, taste it, smell it, or even see it.

It's not like selling a Rolls-Royce where you can get the client to sit in the car and to feel the supple leather of the seats supporting them perfectly in their driving position as they whizz along the road at sixty miles an hour, with the only sound they can hear being the ticking of the beautifully designed analogue clock occupying pride of place on the dashboard.

That's tangible. That's something people can equate to value based on their life experience of driving other vehicles. So how do you sell an intangible like a service, particularly a service that's maybe only used once or twice in a client's lifetime? Well, it's your job to educate your potential client, over and over if necessary, to ensure they make the right decision when it comes to selecting the best solicitor (you) to help them buy or sell their home.

Yet to be successful, you must do things very differently to your competition. And generally speaking, you must start your client's education journey much earlier on in the process; well before they are even thinking about selling their home. And when you do this effectively, you'll be the only obvious choice in your marketplace. But to do so, will require you to operate in a way that's almost counter opposite to your competition, and that can be a lonely journey.

Are you willing to take some risks in order to benefit from the rewards which can be reaped from doing so? I appreciate asking solicitors to take risks is against their nature, however to get ahead and finally make a good living for yourself, you need to make one or two different moves. Even better, because of the general conservative nature of law firms, it will take a long time before your competition catches on, and when they do so, you will have already established a very healthy head-start, and at best, they can only ever be perceived as a poor imitation of you and the great value service you're already offering.

The First Step On A Lonely Journey

One of the most overlooked points in legal land is that solicitors are immune to the fact their clients move house, on average, every 23 years! When you're in the day-to-day business of buying and selling homes for people, your knowledge in this area and how to navigate the stresses and strains of doing so, is incredibly valuable. However, such specialist knowledge, is unknown by your prospective clients and without it, they fall prey to pitfalls, difficulties and manipulations, (such as choosing your competition for example!).

When you demonstrate this knowledge to your potential clients (which to you may seem very simple and straight-forward), it will likely be perceived as a complete revelation and incredibly useful to help them navigate the third most stressful thing they can go through in their lives. Think about in-depth answers to the following and how you can position yourself in front of your client to assist them as much as possible:

1) What should a potential home buyer or seller consider when choosing a conveyancer?
2) Why cheap lawyers' fees might be more expensive than clients think.
3) Why choosing the wrong solicitor can cause a client to miss out on the home of their dreams.
4) The importance of providing the buyer with up-front information to prevent a possible sale from falling through and your client losing the home of their dreams.
5) How to choose the right solicitor to handle the sale, and why choosing the cheapest will leave you unhappy, frustrated and potentially losing the home of your dreams.
6) The pitfalls of conveyancing and how they can bring in an expert to fight their corner for them.

7) The most important considerations to bear in mind when selling your home to help your client achieve the best possible price.

One thing which needs to be said is that people are all very different. They make different decisions based on the same information and some approach decision-making from a point of view of logic, versus using their emotions to make the decision for them. What most don't realise however, is that almost all people make emotional decisions first, and then justify that decision using logic.

This might seem an alien concept to solicitors who are used to observing their client's situations from a calm, independent, non-emotionally-involved point of view, but when it comes to making decisions in their own lives, such as what car they drive, what furniture they buy or the home they live in, they're invariably making emotional decisions first, backed up by logic afterwards. So, it's important to help your clients by providing them with the right information to logically justify the emotional decision of choosing you as their preferred solicitor.

Why Are You Telling Me This?

The secret shortcut to overcoming potential client objections to paying higher fees is for those objections to not raise their ugly head in the first place! And the only way to prevent those objections being raised, which stops a client from automatically working with you (because they're all terrified of getting screwed), is to provide a customer education and nurturing journey ahead of time that will prove yourself to your client so in the client's mind, you become extremely desirable to work with and the client willingly does business with you, rather than having to tempt clients by cutting fees.

So, whilst your competition focuses solely on trying to win the business on the initial phone call, with the power of technology and a little bit of creative writing and video time, you'll be laying the foundations to win the business before your client even thinks about moving home.

Look at the needs of your inexperienced client, then provide the content, educational materials, and technology to regularly keep them updated, so that when they come to sell or buy, you'll be at the forefront of their mind as they'll already have had more tangible insights into your service levels than those of your competition.

#4 Make Your Client The Absolute Priority

Most law firms think they make their clients the priority in their business, however the client's experience usually tells a very different story. Especially in conveyancing. Think about the numerous obligations you have when acting on behalf of a buyer or seller; to the Law Society, Solicitors Regulation Authority, the Land Registry and the mortgage lender, and even your professional indemnity insurance company. Unfortunately, the client comes very far down the list of priorities and when the number of clients increases, keeping in regular contact with them becomes an impossibility.

Yet, the advent of technology can support you in keeping your client informed of what's going on. We're not talking about your case management system; there's a plethora of other bits of technology that can help reduce your workload and keep your client updated at the same time.

The best way to implement this is to sit down and really think about the client's journey in buying or selling a home. And don't just consider the part of the journey that the client goes through with you – it's not a process that occurs in isolation. There are all sorts of hoops a client has to jump through – everything from dealing with estate agents, mortgage brokers, surveyors, mortgage lenders, even down to the council tax and utilities. Are there any parts of the process where you can add value along the way to your client's journey? I'm sure when you think about it practically, there are.

We've touched on a couple of points throughout this guide so far, however taking the bull by the horns by beginning to produce content for your clients, or working in partnership with a number of other service providers who can make a difference to your client can not only make their journey far more pleasurable, it can also be hugely profitable for all involved. When you position the client at the centre of the process and start making decisions around giving them the best service possible (at a healthy fee level for you and your company of course), you'll start to come up with all sorts of ideas that can be useful for your client.

For example, think about the number of times a client must show their identification documents to the various different parties involved. It's not uncommon for them to have to show it 3+ times which is crazy when you consider it could be shown once to their legal representatives, who could confirm their client's identity to all parties as part of their service offering. This might seem like a small detail but think of the delays encountered when a client has to arrange to physically go and see someone to prove their identity, when there are so many online services available that will do this almost instantly for very low cost.

How about the coordination process between the mortgage broker, mortgage valuer, and the estate agent? Well, some will say that's the agent or client's job, but is it really? Is there any value you can offer here that would make your client's moving experience effortless?

The Biggest Lost Opportunity In Conveyancing

Here's a huge hidden secret that most lawyers overlook in building their business which really does sort the wheat from the chaff. It's the opportunity to cross-sell your client a greater suite of services, therefore increasing the average customer spend with your firm. If you've taken the time to work out how much it costs your company to acquire a new client, the difference between winning a new client for a house purchase, updating someone's will and providing them with guidance around protecting their wealth through the use of a Trust for example, you'll know that if you can remove the costs of acquiring a new client for two or more of your additional services by selling them all to the same client, your profit margins should go through the roof.

Except there's one sticking point. And it's the client's experience of using the law firm in the first place. A new client goes to a conveyancer to buy or sell their home, and receives such a dreadful service, that they vow with all their might never to do business with that company ever again. The result? Well, not only has the firm lost the opportunity to sell more services and make more money, that client will be so angry and upset due to all the delays involved and the fact the solicitor wouldn't return any of their phone calls, that they tell at least 6 other people about the shocking service they received (or worse, leaves a one-star Trustpilot review telling the world how unfortunate they were). The leveraged power of the internet can work both for or against us all in business.

Opportunity lost. Fees lost. Future business in the client's network lost. Still, at least you can always cut fees to win more business…and so the negative downward death-spiral of a lack of profitability in your company continues.

A Helping Hand

I did say at the start of this guide that I was going to be brutally honest with you and therefore I won't apologise for bringing all this to your attention. A lot of lawyers will argue with me and tell me that it doesn't apply to their business and that they do things differently.

However, I'll bet that if we were to honestly interview 100 of their clients, we'd find tens of thousands of possible income left on the table. Don't believe me? Go to the Money Saving Expert website and read some of the comments in the forums to see how the house buying and selling public perceive solicitors and conveyancers in general based on their experiences of poor service levels received. It's a shame that solicitors are not getting the recognition they deserve when this part of the process is so easy to fix.

We recognise that sometimes it's not easy to step back from the coal-face and take a holistic high-level view of your business to implement different changes, which is why we offer pro-active lawyers a free 30-minute consultation to really understand the problems they're facing, and how we might be able to help solve them for their clients.

If you'd like to take advantage of our FREE, no-obligation consultations, just go to

www.WiggyWam.co.uk/FreeSolicitorConsultation and we'll see if there's a good match to assist you.

#5 Help Your Clients Choose The Right Solicitor

A lot of solicitors don't realise the impact of this one – which is crazy because we think it's an absolute MUST-DO when it comes to helping your client sell or buy their dream home. We've touched on a couple of points as to why this is so essential, however we're going to take a deeper dive into this right now, so you can overcome what I personally think is the biggest obstacle standing in the way of clients achieving their dreams, and in turn, you are handsomely rewarded for your efforts.

A solicitor's job is to effectively transfer the legal title of a property from the seller to the buyer, without any mistakes that could cause either party problems in the future. If you think about the client's mindset of buying a home, they want to make sure that when they're living there, they don't have the ramblers walking past their kitchen window on a Sunday morning, or that the Highways Authority plan to run a new motorway through their back garden, or that there's going to be a new nightclub opening up three doors away and they're going to hear drunken revellers spilling out of the club at 2am on a Saturday and Sunday morning!

This is an essential part of the solicitor's job. Your clients also want to be sure that when it comes time to move on, there won't be any complications with the Legal Title that prevents them from selling.

Another important point in the solicitor's role is to handle the large volume of funds used in the sale or purchase of their new home which come from the mortgage lender, and the client's own funds. If solicitors are unscrupulous, clients fear they could run off with their money, leaving them high and dry and without the home of their dreams!

In short, the solicitor's job is both high pressure and carries a lot of responsibility which most people aren't aware of. They just want the deal completed asap, so they can live in their dream home. And who can blame them?

So, let's look at exactly what you'll be doing to assist them in the purchase of their new home. Firstly, as we touched on previously, the back-and-forth process of raising enquiries drains a lot of time in the transaction, and more importantly, I'm sure you'll agree that most of the other solicitors you deal with, aren't exactly proactive. This is where the expertise of a good solicitor comes in handy when chasing other parties to get them to talk to one another!

Secondly, you'll usually get your client to pay for searches on the property they're buying. Local authorities can be notoriously slow in responding to searches. Depending upon how efficient the local authority is, will determine whether they'll issue the information within a couple of days or weeks from their computer system, allow a representative to go directly to the council to do a 'hand search' to speed up the process, or whether the information required is quite literally sat in a 'biscuit tin' and it will take several weeks for someone to sift through all the papers to give you the responses you require. However, what a lot of solicitors don't do, is order the searches early enough in the process due to some unfounded fear that this might actually fall foul of their professional duties under the regulatory bodies.

If a solicitor is overly cautious in ordering searches earlier on in the process, they can settle their nervousness by simply asking (themselves and), their client the following question:

"Would you like us to get a good head start on all the legal work by ordering your searches right now for the nominal cost of £200+VAT which could save us 6-8 weeks of waiting around if we leave it until much later in the process, or are you happy to wait a longer period of time for the searches to come back where the risk of losing your buyer/dream home is a lot higher as all parties get frustrated because the deal is not yet exchanged?"

Basically, you're asking them to 'pay away the pain' by making a small investment in the purchase of their dream home which may not be recovered if the sale falls through, but which could save them weeks, or months, of gut-wrenching stress and frustration waiting on something that could have been done a lot earlier on in the process.

For those who will argue against this stating they have an obligation to their client and their regulators to not spend client funds unnecessarily, I will respond by saying this is a very short-sighted approach which lacks empathy and fails to consider the stress and pressure your clients are going through when making the biggest financial and emotional decision of their life.

In short, you DO have an obligation to your client, and that's to make sure the deal goes through as quickly as possible, as stress-free as possible, and with a greater level of certainty that isn't going to leave your client with a big professional services bill at the end of the process purely because they lost their buyer or dream home because all parties became so frustrated with delays (and/or lack of communication), they pulled out of the deal.

Incidentally, one of the reasons solicitors give for not ordering the searches earlier in the process is because of their cost. Having investigated this area fully, I can confirm the reason why reason searches are so costly; it's because of the number of middlemen who each add their own little margin which the client ultimately ends up paying for.

To overcome this obstacle, we recommend speaking to us directly as we have enrolled the largest search provider into our mission to remove the barriers people face when moving home, and they are keen to support us and our clients in not only providing great value-for-money searches, but also speeding up the process significantly by using a very unique process exclusively available through us. We can talk more about this on the free 30-minute, no-obligation consultation by going to www.WiggyWam.co.uk/FreeSolicitorsConsultation and we'll see if there's a good match to help you to help your clients.

Now we've covered the top 5 tips, we'd like to share some more value with you by highlighting some of the common mistakes home buyers and sellers make along the way. Feel free to use this information as a guide to assist you in helping your clients as much as possible.

The 3 Most Common Mistakes Made By Buyers & Sellers And How You Can Easily Avoid Them

Sadly, when it comes to buying or selling a home, too many buyers and sellers make simple mistakes which cost them dearly. If you're not careful, you could follow in their footsteps and end up helping them fall well short of their goal.

But don't worry – we're here to help.

We've put together a list of the 3 most common mistakes made by buyers and sellers – as well as easy-to-follow tips on how to avoid them. Use this expert information to help guide and support your clients as much as possible and to make more money in the process.

#1 Leaving It All To Someone Else

Far and away the most common mistake buyers and sellers make is leaving the whole process to someone else. We see it all too often - we've honestly lost count of how many people we've come across who have made this error. You see, there's not a lot of reliable information out there for people to refer to that is backed by decades of experience in the property industry. In fact, if we're honest, most stuff we read on the internet is just copied and pasted garbage from blogs written by people who don't even own their own home!

Most people move home, on average, every 28 years and that's a long time between transactions to be familiar with all the headaches, bear-traps, and hurdles you have to negotiate. As a consequence, most people try to leave the process to others (estate agents, mortgage brokers, and solicitors), without fully understanding what these different parties do for their money and how they can help, or hinder, progress.

Let's be honest, if you don't know about something, it's very easy to be taken advantage of. Think about taking your car to the garage with a problem and the mechanic sucks air through his teeth with a concerned look on his face before telling you the "flux capacitor" needs changing. If you don't know any different, chances are you're going to be taken advantage of, or at the very least, end up with a bunch of headaches that could have easily been solved earlier in the process had you known what to expect.

So, how do you go about learning all you need to know to protect yourself in your buying or selling journey, without having to spend years training to be a solicitor, mortgage broker, estate agent, and surveyor? Well, reading this eBook is a great place to start. Knowing where things could fall down points to areas where problems may exist, so you can be better prepared to deal with them.

The next step is to continue your education journey through the WiggyWam learning library and you can register for an account for FREE. The learning library covers a lot of the topics presented here in greater detail, as well as many others outside the scope of this guide. Go to www.wiggywam.co.uk/learn to get started. We provide tons of resources to make the journey to buying and selling utopia a reality.

Finally, I recommend clients involve themselves heavily in the transaction process. Everybody else isn't going to look after their best interests as well as they themselves will. This means they must take an active interest in the progress of their deal and do as much work up front as they can.

If they're a seller, it means gathering all the information necessary to give a buyer confidence in buying their property. They should secure the LPE1 information pack from the freehold management company if you're selling a leasehold property. They should complete the sellers pack nice and early in the process, so the solicitor isn't chasing for outstanding information to complete the deal (WiggyWam can help you with this).

If they're a buyer, they need to get their finances in place early and sell their own property if they have one. They should take an active interest in reading the survey and valuation report and get their identification documents and relevant information to their broker and solicitor in good time. Updates to the estate agent regularly helps keep everyone updated. Nothing is more important than making sure everyone knows what's going on as its usually the lack of communication that makes people nervous and want to pull out of the deal.

#2 Choosing The Wrong Representatives

Choosing the wrong representatives is another common mistake and its right up there with leaving it all to someone else in terms of the amount of time, effort, and money it costs buyers and sellers to move home. It's such an easy mistake to avoid, but it happens WAY more often than it should.

It's worth investing the time, effort, and money into getting the right team on board. Think about buying a used car – would you go to the smooth talking 'Del Boy' look-a-like in his sheepskin coat who'll say anything to sell you a car without a warranty?

Or would you prefer to buy from a reputable dealer who has taken the time to do a multi-point inspection on the vehicle and who will offer you a warranty for your peace of mind? You'd be right in thinking that the second option here is more expensive, but what's the cost of buying a car without a warranty, only to have something major go wrong with it once you've driven it off the forecourt? (Take it from someone whose father spent most of his life in the used car game; you need to be very careful about who you trust in the car as well as the home-buying process).

We encourage clients to invest their hard-earned money in the right representatives to help them buy or sell the most expensive asset they'll likely own in their life as it will stack the odds firmly in their favour.

If you need help in finding or recommending the right people to work with, we can assist. Email us on HappyToHelp@wiggywam.co.uk

#3 Not Protecting The Downside

On the surface, this mistake might not seem as common as the first two we've outlined – but that doesn't make it any less harmful. In fact, it could be the costliest out of the three – an error that could see your clients throw away thousands of pounds and hours of their life, leaving them further away from their goal than when they first started.

As with most things in life, people mistakenly believe that 'it'll never happen to them' despite the horror stories you hear from others. They always think they'll be the ones that get away with it, so they think they don't need to worry about what might go wrong. We see this in all areas of people's lives, from their health to their financial position, and even choosing the wrong partner (in business and in marriage).

But you see, when it comes to buying or selling a home, there's a lot that could go wrong and if you're one of the 20-40% of homeowners who fail to sell their home when they put it up for sale, you could cost yourself thousands in the process with agents or solicitors fees. As a buyer, you could suffer the same fate having paid out thousands to surveyors, brokers and lawyers, just to not buy your dream home.

So, it's vital to protect the downside in any deal and for the cost of doing so, it's a complete no-brainer to put a costs-indemnity insurance in place before a client starts their buying and selling journey. Trust me when I tell you that very few agents, solicitors, or brokers know it's possible to do this, and consequently, they'll probably tell you it's not possible or it doesn't exist, but nothing could be further from the truth.

Quite honestly, if you could invest £100 which would recover any professional fees up to £1,800 spent in trying to buy or sell a home, wouldn't it be worth it? To me, it makes perfect sense to do so and prevents a bad situation from turning worse should you have to pull out of a deal.

If you can't find a reliable costs-indemnity insurance company to work with, email us on HappyToHelp@wiggywam.co.uk and we'll do our best to help you out.

3 Insider Secrets Which Can Help Your Clients Buy Or Sell Your Home In As Little As 10 Weeks

At WiggyWam, we've got our fingers on the pulse of the property industry, and we've picked up a secret or two during our 25+years in the business. Here are a few gems you can use to help your clients buy or sell their home in as little as 10 weeks (less than half the time solicitors are quoting currently).

#1 Get Them To Do The Work

Not many lawyers realise this – but actually getting your clients to do the work rather than mistakenly trying to rely on others to do it for them will drastically reduce the amount of time it takes to buy or sell a property. We've already covered what a lot of this looks like earlier in this eBook, but here's a quick reminder:

- As a buyer, make sure they get their Decision In Principle (DiP) in place for their mortgage (if not a cash buyer), and bank statements to show proof of deposit. They'll need ID documents to prove who they are. Also, if they need to sell a property to buy the next one, they'll need to do everything below.

- As a seller, they'll need to complete a seller's pack ideally before the property goes on the market and get any other necessary information together, like your LPE1 leasehold information pack from the freehold management company if they're selling a flat or other leasehold property. For the cost of it, it's also worthwhile your client considering getting a condition survey for their home so any buyer is fully informed on exactly what they're buying, as well as putting the searches in place too. True, the searches may only be valid for 3+ months, but assuming they've listed their property at a reasonable price, then 3 months should be more than sufficient. By being transparent, they'll greatly reduce the likelihood of any sale agreed on their home falling through or a buyer pulling out because the property is not what they were expecting it to be. We've included a checklist of the documents they'll need to have in place towards the end of this eBook, so please don't overlook this.

I cannot stress the importance of doing this work upfront nice and early, even before considering selling or buying a property as failure to do so can cost thousands of pounds. The trouble for most people is that they don't know any different, so they ignore these important points, only to endure endless delays later on or end up in a situation that costs them thousands, when they could have taken pro-active steps to organise themselves earlier in the process.

The tips we're sharing here come from 25+ years' experience in the industry and working with literally thousands of people up and down the country to help them buy and sell property, so ignore them at your peril! By doing the work earlier in the process (work that will have to be done in any event), you remove the time delays in the back-and-forth process between all parties to the deal.

The more delays encountered, the higher risk there is in a buyer getting overly frustrated and pulling out, leaving your client with a big legal bill and potentially losing the home of their dreams. The same goes for any buyer who procrastinates on the purchase and incurs the wrath of the seller losing their patience who then pulls out of the deal. Be serious. Be committed. And Do. The. Work.

#2 Get Costs Indemnity Insurance In Place

This is something buyers and sellers are always shocked to hear when we tell them about it – but once we do, their surprise quickly turns to delight as they realise how much money it can save them should their potential deal fall through. It's a fact of buying or selling property that as many as 2 in every 5 deals will fall through, and with such a high percentage of transactions falling apart, doesn't it make sense to protect your clients financially?

When you consider that abortive legal fees can be £500 +VAT, the valuation can cost £300-700+VAT, a survey (Homebuyers Report or Building Survey) £600-£2,000+VAT, and broker fees £200+VAT or more, then costs can quickly escalate. When someone pulls out of the deal, all professional advisors working for the client still get paid, but the client is the one left out of pocket. Surely it makes sense to underwrite the potential losses, so if the deal falls apart, your client's costs are covered?

Think of it like an insurance policy against your home or car. You put insurance in place so that if, God forbid, you have a fire at home, or an accident in your car, someone else carries the costs of putting it right. The costs could be several thousand pounds, and you pay a small premium each year to cover your potential losses.

A costs indemnity insurance underwrites your client's professional costs in much the same way. They pay a small premium to protect their interests, and if the sale or purchase is aborted, they simply make a claim and get their costs refunded. To me, this is one of the best things you can do to protect your client and I only wish it had been available years ago when I first started buying property. It would have saved me so much money over the years.

The best guidance I can give is for your client to get this in place before they start their buying or selling journey. The peace of mind is more than worth the small sum they'll pay to cover themselves and relieves a lot of stress should the deal fall apart. They simply fill out a form and recover their costs – one less thing to worry about!

#3 Choose The Right Solicitors

This is something we're keen to share after 25 years in the industry – but it's far from common knowledge, even among other property professionals, estate agents, solicitors, brokers, property portals, and property training platforms. The reason for this I believe is simply lack of experience. Most people will only buy or sell one property in their lifetime, so their experience doesn't count for much when advising others on what's involved.

Ask your friends and family what their recent moving experience was like. Virtually everyone you talk to will have some horror story to share with you and its usually centred around choosing the wrong solicitor. They'll tell you that they didn't return their phone calls or emails. They'll tell you that there were delays and no-one knew why or what was going on. They'll tell you that things were left to the last minute and forms which should have been sent out weeks ago or information that should have been asked for at the start of the process didn't happen. Or they'll tell you that they had to pay their solicitor £800+VAT for not actually moving. Risky business!

There's a world of difference between having theoretical knowledge of how something works, and practical experience of going through it yourself several times. Unfortunately, most people involved in home buying and selling haven't gone through the process more than a couple of times themselves, and it shows.

I literally shudder when I think back to my time as an estate agent and how incredibly naïve I was. Yes, I was well meaning and enthusiastic, but I was little more than a key-holder and in certain circumstances, a spare part to negotiations. If I had to face my younger estate-agent-self now, with all my years of experience, I'd literally make mincemeat out of myself! And I thought I was great at my job!

The point is, most estate agents and solicitors I've interviewed the length and breadth of the country, having trained thousands of people in the fine art of buying and selling property, lack a lot of expertise. They won't like me saying that of course, but the good ones stand out head and shoulders above the rest. Whenever you meet an estate agent or other property professional who has significant experience in buying and selling (as opposed for and on behalf of other people), you'll instantly be able to tell the difference.

We always suggest to clients, if you're wondering whether or not the solicitor you're thinking about using is the right person for the job, ask them how quickly they can complete the deal. If they're quoting anything longer than 10 weeks, I'd want to know why. Ask them if they are prepared to sign a Service Level Agreement (SLA), which states they will return all calls and emails within 24 hours (excluding the weekend), or they'll reduce their fees each time it happens. See what response you get. Will they agree to it? Or will they start getting a little hot under the collar and tell you all the reasons why it's sometimes not possible to return a call or email within 24 hours and that "they'll do their best…"

Put simply, there's no single role in the home buying or selling journey that's more essential to get right. Choose the right solicitor and your journey will be a lot easier. Get the wrong one and you may as well set fire to a thousand pounds and book yourself in for some therapy to recover from the emotional trauma of the experience (please don't actually set fire to the cash; its illegal – I'm just using the visual image as an illustration of what you'll metaphorically be doing! Booking the therapy might not be a bad idea however…).

Finally, we say to clients if you're struggling to find the right solicitor for the job, or you want to take advantage of an exclusive offer we're running for a very limited time only, to grab a FREE Seller's Pack for your client's property sale, then we can do our best to help you at WiggyWam. Just email us on HappyToHelp@WiggyWam.co.uk with the subject line: 'Free Seller's Pack' and we'll get back to you.

For solicitors, we know how hard you work and whilst you're good at your job, you sometimes feel let down by others in a chain who don't perform. We think that's bad practice and deserves to be stamped out from the industry. We also feel you deserve to make more money for the job you do whilst removing the mundane and common-place hurdles that so often prevent property deals from moving as quickly as they should.

To offer you as much value as possible, we provide forward-thinking solicitors (who want to know how to effortlessly improve their processes, win more business and improve their fees), a free 30-minute consultation to show you how. If you'd like to know more, claim your complimentary consultation here:

www.WiggyWam.co.uk/FreeSolicitorsConsultation

The TRUTH About The Property Industry And Why Most Buyers And Sellers Fail To Buy Their Dream Home Without Stress, Headaches And Financial Heartache.

Have you ever tried to do something difficult without help? It could be something as simple as trying to move a heavy piece of furniture – like a desk – all by yourself. You probably knew at the back of your mind it was better to ask a friend, colleague, or family member for help – but you became impatient and gave it a go, to see if you could do it yourself.

Sadly, shortly after trying, it became clear that you just couldn't do it. The desk was WAY too heavy. Not only did you knock over the nearby lamp, but you've now got a stabbing pain in your lower back… and the desk is still stuck right where it was.

If only you'd asked for help…

Well, the truth is the property industry is a lot like that. Although instead of a desk, I want you to imagine trying to raise the Titanic from the bottom of the ocean. On your own. Without diving equipment, floatation aids, or a ship! It can be very difficult – or even impossible – for clients to attempt to buy their dream home without any independent assistance from someone experienced who wants to help fight their corner for them.

Unfortunately, clients feel trying to buy their dream home is more like raising the Titanic than moving a simple piece of furniture. And the consequences are far more costly than hurting their lower back or putting a scratch on the wall.

Not only could your clients cost themselves thousands of pounds in the process, but they could also set themselves back weeks or even months on their journey. Frustratingly, they could end up further away from achieving their desired outcome than they are right now.

Sadly, this is something that happens all too often to buyers and sellers. Instead of seeking expert help, they try to go it alone and fall well short of achieving their goals.

That's why it's imperative they ask for expert advice to help achieve their goals. And in the property industry, there's no one better than WiggyWam. We have over 25 years of experience in the industry – during which time we've helped literally thousands of people on their journey to buying property.

We can help your clients avoid the common pitfalls, steer clear of the costly mistakes, and buy their dream home in the shortest possible timeframe. Why risk your clients losing thousands of pounds to not buy their dream home, or put them in hospital because of the stress when things go badly wrong, when you can use our expertise and proven systems to help them to buy or sell quickly? To find out how we can help, get in touch with us for a free, no-obligation consultation.

Claim Your FREE No-Obligation 30-Minute Consultation And We'll Help Your Clients To Buy Or Sell Their Home Quickly

Thank you for taking the time to read this eBook – we hope you found the information helpful, and you can use what you've learned to help your clients move home with the least amount of headaches or problems.

If you're truly serious about helping them without falling prey to all the bear-traps along the way, then we have excellent news. For a limited time only, we're offering you a free, no-obligation session with one of our property industry experts.

During your complimentary 30-minute session, we'll discuss your current situation, what your goals are and how we can help you achieve them using our proven system.

We'll also cover a stack of valuable information together, including…

How you can help your clients buy (or sell) their home in under 10 weeks, what you should never do when going through the process, and how to avoid all the most common mistakes that buyers, sellers, and solicitors make which sabotages their success.

There's no cost or obligation to move forwards with our service afterwards if you feel like it's not for you. It's simply a free information session designed to educate you and provide value to you in advance.

To claim your free consultation or find out more information about this limited-time offer, all you have to do is visit the link below.

www.WiggyWam.Cco.uk/FreeSolicitorsConsultation

Checklist Of Up-Front Information Required To Help Your Clients Sell In Under 10 Weeks

1) Sellers Certificate.
2) TA6 Form duly completed.
3) TA10 Form duly completed.
4) Land Registry Title Deeds.
5) Land Registry Plan, indicating responsibility for each boundary on the plan.
6) Energy Performance Certificate (EPC).
7) Recent Electrical inspection report.
8) Recent Gas Safety Certificate & Boiler Servicing/Installation Certificates.
9) Building Regulations Certificate for any recent work carried out.
10) FENSA Certificate if you've had windows changed since April 2002.
11) Installation certificates for solar panels (if applicable).
12) Recent Timber & Damp report.
13) Condition survey – A pre-marketing inspection report on your home (email us on HappyToHelp@wiggywam.co.uk for more information)

14) Copies of any approved Planning Permission and copies of plans etc. for any work you may have had done on the property recently (extensions/conversions, conservatory additions).

15) Copies of any conservation area approvals for any work done on your property if you live in a conservation area.

16) Copies of any listed buildings approval if your property happens to be a listed building.

17) Identify the location of the water Stop Tap, Gas & Electric Meters and gas shut off valve.

18) Details of any rights of way or other easements (legal rights granted in favour of another) across your land.

19) Searches pack – if you'd like help getting this together at a cost-effective price, email us on HappyToHelp@wiggywam.co.uk for more information.

Please note: The above information is not exhaustive and your solicitors may ask for further information not listed here. However, this will usually arm them with sufficient documents to fast-track your legal process.

In Review

Now, how was that? Did you learn a thing or two about structuring a lead magnet and what information to include to be as helpful as possible? Also, did you notice any particular emotions coming up for you as you read the report? Ask yourself, if you were a solicitor reading it, what actions would you take as a result?

We hope you'll agree that when something is spelt out in black and white, it can be pretty confronting and that can make us feel uncomfortable, or even downright angry. And that's a good thing.

Why you ask?

Think about it this way, when you're essentially asking someone to do something, you need them to have an incentive to do it. And sometimes that incentive can be as simple as getting out of an uncomfortable emotional state. They can exit that uncomfortable emotional state by taking action to book a call.

Did you notice we outlined some problems, offered some solutions, and then offered more value with a call-to-action? It doesn't have to be any more complicated than that.

CHAPTER THREE

CREATING A SECRET ARMY OF DIGITAL SALESMEN

This book wouldn't be complete without reference to one of the most essential skills you can learn if you truly want to transform your agency and make it worth a fortune. It's also the key to automating a lot of what you're doing and building an army of silent assassins who kneecap your competition so they don't ever get a look-in on the instructions you really want to win.

If you're excited to know what that skill is, it's the skill of copywriting, or as its informally known, salesmanship in print, or salesmanship <u>multiplied</u> through print.

Most agents are naturally pretty good at sales but taking that skill and making it work on paper is a whole different ball game. But when you master it, you'll find yourself being able to work a ton of different angles which hook customers into your world, get them excited and more importantly, get them to take action.

This is why we talked about the emotional states above. Copywriting is not only making your reader feel understood but giving them access to solutions they need to solve their problems. You can instantly see how this differs from talking about features and benefits, or merely describing the product or service you offer and giving your clients a price.

With copywriting, you're creating the hook, which is the bait, or pattern interrupt required to get your intended client to enter into your world. Think about this for a moment, most people are incredibly busy and they're subject to a million distractions. Email, instant messaging, phone calls, text messages,

Netflix, snail mail, social media, the news, the radio and a whole host of other demands, responsibilities, and things that require someone's attention. And it can be overwhelming to the point where most people's attention span has been reduced to less than 10 seconds before the next interruption comes their way.

BUT, at the same time, each and every one of us is walking around with a 'perfect vision' of who we should be in our minds and contrasting our day-to-day life against this perfect vision. Where there's a difference between the two, (and there almost always is), our human minds exploit the disparity which leaves us feeling upset, frustrated, and sad that we haven't yet achieved the perfect version of ourselves that we hold in our minds eye, we then start looking for solutions to these problems of not being where we want to be.

For example, you might think you're overweight and need to lose a few pounds to feel better about yourself. If you walk past a newsstand or scroll on Insta to see scantily clad people living the dream, the comparison with your own internal world makes you feel uncomfortable. So, the natural thing to do is take steps to do something about it. Maybe you join a gym or go running, but after a while when you haven't yet achieved this perfect version, you give up and go back to the way things were. And then your problem gets agitated again when you watch the latest episode of Selling Sunset, and you think you really must do something about your weight loss, and around and around and around you go again.

So, if you were in the weight loss industry, you would need to use some form of hook to bring these people into your world, so you can offer them a genuine solution to help them solve their weight loss challenge. This might be a Facebook Advert to interrupt their mindless scrolling with a picture which stands out and a headline that reads 'Tired of not knowing the <u>real</u> secret to losing weight? Click here to find out more'

Now, depending upon the amount of pain someone may be in, they may decide to click on the advert to find out more.

Can you see how this works? The advert interrupts their thinking pattern, agitates a pain point, and gets the client to take action to enter the online world of a potential solution provider, (so they can bring that person into their selling environment). And this selling environment is where the magic happens.

It's a bit like seeing an advert on a billboard for a fancy watch; you're made aware of the offer, but you wouldn't necessarily buy the watch from a street-vendor selling out of a suitcase underneath the billboard. But you would most likely enter a local shop or jewellers to check out the watch, and if you're satisfied, you'll whip out your credit card and bag yourself a deal.

Agitating The Pain

Now in the process of moving home, you already know your prospects are going to feel plenty of pain, so it's your job to protect them from as much of it as possible. But unfortunately, the way of the world is, you must make them feel that pain a little before they will ever take action to do something about it. And if you're ever going to be a champion estate agent, you know you'll need to make your client experience a little bit of this pain or discomfort BEFORE they instruct your competition who won't be quite so considerate of their needs.

So the point of the copywriting process is to help create mental imagery in the mind of your potential client, which will cause them to experience emotions which are uncomfortable enough that they call you because they know they're going to need your help. However, this can be a double-edged sword and you have to do this in such a way that doesn't frighten the client to death, but also doesn't bore them to death either! It's more profitable to work with clients who are alive…

And this can be the biggest challenge – agents want to be loved and want to help their clients as much as possible, which is noble, but you must learn from the best copywriters in the world who will tell you that without making your target client feel some emotion, they're never going to get off the sofa, pick up the phone that's charging in the kitchen, and send you an email, or call you and have that conversation. They'll simply dismiss it by saying "I must remember to do that…" and then promptly forget about it as they wander off back to doing whatever they were doing before they were interrupted. If you lose that opportunity to get them to take action, you'll likely lose them for good.

This is why you'll hear a lot of people talk about lead magnets and using them in your marketing process. They're good 'bait' to use to give to your prospect in exchange for their email address. You're providing value in exchange for something equally valuable, their contact details. Because once you have them, you can begin to build a relationship with them, and over time, drive them towards a pre-determined action you want them to take – make a call, email you, or instruct you to sell their property for them.

Learning copywriting is not something that can be mastered overnight and can take years if you want to become amazing at it. Hiring someone may be possible, but be warned, there's a huge difference between the best and the rest. Here's 11 top tips to help you if you decide to make a go of copywriting to boost your business:

1) **Define your objective** – who are you marketing to and what do you want them to do at the end of it? Going from an advert to instructing you to sell their property might be a stretch too far but getting them to give you their email address so you can build a relationship via your nurturing program is a sensible first step.

2) **What's the exchange?** – Work out what value you can offer in exchange for the step you're asking your potential client to take. Do they get a free eBook, PDF, video series, or consultation call? Define the value you're giving them so you can find the best words to describe your offer.

3) **Don't be boring** – Key point, if your client dies of boredom whilst they're reading your advert, or copy, you won't sell them a thing! Your text should begin to build mental pictures in people's minds that are emotive and will get a response. Make you target feel something, anything, whilst they're reading. Just don't be boring!

4) **Know the difference between short form and long form copy** – Your collection of words to sell something is called copy. Different mediums require different copy. For example, an email would be short form copy, but a sales page is long form. Interestingly, long

form copy outsells short form by a significant margin, but it has to be used in the right medium. A long form email is not going to work, but a short form email driving people to your long form sales page could work wonders.

5) **Study the greats** – Most of the best advertising and marketing executives have all studied copywriting, and in particular Direct Response Marketing (you know the letters you get in the post telling you a story before getting you to buy something). It's the most powerful way to really move the needle with your sales, if you know what you're doing. Study the work of Claude Hopkins in his book Scientific Advertising and David Ogilvy in his book Ogilvy on Advertising.

6) **Measure your results** – The one thing copywriting has the power to do that most advertising does not, is give you a methodology to measure your results. If you get this right, not only do you know who you are marketing to, because you have their email address, you can even see how many people have opened your email, where they've clicked and whether they've gone on to read your sales page or any other action they've taken. A bit Big Brother? Maybe, but its powerful. Insanely powerful. Contrast that to an advert in the paper or on the television where you have no idea how many people have seen it or if they're taking any other action as a result. When you know who is taking action and who's not, you can design a different campaign with greater appeal to your active prospects.

7) **Build Your 'Swipe File'** – a swipe file is a marketing term which describes a file of previous adverts or copy which you found interesting, or it provoked an emotional reaction, and you want to use it as a guide in building your own copy. This used to be a paper folder, but as time has moved on, you can use Google Drive, or simply bookmark webpages of interest. Start building one out as it's amazing what you can learn from others, and sometimes a simple sentence or phrase can bring multiplied results in your advertising efforts.

8) **Always split test** – a split test means you are testing two different versions of the same advert or body copy to determine which works best. With the wonders of modern technology, you can split test two different versions 'live' as it directs your online traffic to one advert

first, and then the next person who comes along sees the second version. You can then see who converts or takes action. If you don't want to use specific tech, you can simply try it by sending two different versions to two select groups of people on your email list and seeing what the results are. You want to use a reasonable sample size though, so make sure it's over 100 people at least to get meaningful results.

9) **Practice, Practice, Practice** – learning any new skill, especially one as high paying as this, will require a lot of practice to get it right. And it's pretty easy to do. You can look at different products and services you find interesting and see how they advertise. Then you can do a mock-up of their advert and change the copy to something more appealing. When you start getting into this, you'll realise that so many products and services are being advertised by agencies who have little clue about copywriting, or about how to drive a response from their target audience. As David Ogilvy famously said: "The direct response guys are the only ones who know what they're doing…"

10) **Come back to it** – Once you've written one or two pieces of copy, let them rest overnight or for a day or two before coming back to it. Sometimes you'll get different flashes of inspiration which will change the whole message, and other times you'll realise it's not saying what you want it to say, or the call to action isn't strong enough. So, give yourself time to revisit it before sending it out to your mailing list.

11) **Always have a call to action** – A call to action, or CTA, is the most overlooked piece in copywriting. There's no point whipping your audience up into a frenzy and then leaving them with a huge anti-climax because they don't know what to do next. They're looking to you for some direction, so make sure you give them some guidance. Click this link, or subscribe now, or forward this email to three friends, are all variations of a call to action. They're powerful, especially if you want to make sales or get people to do something else.

Replication Is The Mother Skill

There's one enormous hidden secret to all the writing and content producing we've been talking about throughout these Volumes, and that's the secret of replication. You see, once you've mapped out a few guides and ideas for solutions to people's problems, you're going to be able to use variations of this content to really turbo-charge your business – and all without having to work a ton of extra hours to generate results, because it'll all be set up to run on autopilot.

Here's what we mean.

You've created a killer guide on how to move home and you've got an email campaign set up which is ticking along nicely and sharing the information with every new person who joins your list. But you decide to take it a step further and expand on the information in the guide by providing a webinar.

So, you take the guide as an outline, quickly craft some slides to form a presentation, invite a bunch of people who you think might be interested and then hit them with your knowledge.

You decide to record the webinar, so your audience can revisit it, but you now also have a second valuable piece of content. Not only could this be repurposed in the form of a podcast, you can also take key snippets from it and use it in online advertising, or little YouTube videos, or even transcribe the whole thing to give another valuable resource for your target audience.

Do you need to do this? No. But look at the exposure you'll get as you work this up and deliver it to your audience. They're going to love you because you just keep coming out with this valuable content and they're getting to consume it for little to no risk. And that massively increases the odds of them coming to work with you when the time is right.

What's even better is the fact that once it's done, its done for life, so you can do the work once, and use that digital asset for forever and a day.

CHAPTER FOUR

SECRETS TO BECOMING
THE AUTHORITY

It is no surprise that the word authority it's largely made up of the word author. This simple statement alone should start pinging some lightbulbs in your mind about where we're going with all of this. Perhaps you can see that becoming a published author would help to give you true status as the go-to expert in your geographical area.

What's that?

Write a book you say?

You do know I failed GCSE English right? How am I meant to do that?

Well take it from someone with mild dyslexia (why is that such a hard word to spell?!) and ADHD, that it's perfectly possible for you to become a published author. But before we get into the how-to, just think for a second how that's going to feel when you're holding YOUR book in your hands? And how special are you going to feel when you're handing a complimentary copy to your prospects during a valuation appointment, and you watch their face light up in amazement that you actually wrote a book that's insightful and helpful with their moving journey.

Think your competition are going to be doing that? Think again!

Think it will stack the odds in your favour of winning more business, AND at higher fees?

You'd be dead right!

Without getting caught up in the overwhelm, let's walk you through some reasons why you'd take on this task and the benefits you can expect for doing so.

Why Become A Published Author?

When you provide valuable information, in the form of a book which has your name on it to potential prospects, you're going to stand out head and shoulders above anyone else. Your prospects will clearly see that you know exactly what you're talking about because by thumbing through the pages of your book, they're getting behind-the-scenes access to your knowledge and expertise.

One of the biggest challenges most agents face is, whilst they might know the job inside out, back to front, and upside down because they've been doing it for 30 years, the client is only exposed to maybe 1-2 hours of their time during a market appraisal before they make that all-important decision about whether or not to place their most valuable asset into the hands of your agency or one of your competitors.

When you become a published author, clients who read your book (or just skim through it), start to understand the depth and breadth of your experience and it gives you the opportunity to tell stories you might not otherwise be able to share due to time restraints, or outline stories which show you and your agency in a very favourable light.

It's a huge credibility boost and will help you to win instructions. Imagine going to a property and during the course of your presentation, pulling a copy of your book out of your briefcase, and handing it to the client with your compliments. Whilst you don't want to distract clients and have them start flicking through the book as you're presenting to them, they'll be asking themselves how many other agents have written a book? The answer is probably not 1 in 1,000.

Not only are you increasing your credibility through the published work you've put in front of your client, but you're also providing huge value to them in a way that no other agent is and acting on the natural human psychological principle of reciprocity, as you've given the client a very valuable asset, the likelihood is, they'll choose to give you their business in return.

Alternatively, your book could be offered as a bonus to help close a deal there and then, or it could be part of your marketing collateral that you give out to people, or you might even decide to charge for it so as not be seen to be giving away all your priceless knowledge and information for free.

Either way, there's plenty of upside, and virtually no downside in writing a book for your key target audience.

However, you could sell yourself short by thinking there's too much work involved in writing a book and you're already too busy with everything else you must do. If that's you, hold fire because we're about to make the whole process as painless and stress-free as possible.

If you want to become the cream of the crop and rise to the top, read on to find out more…

Mapping Out Your Book

Before you begin to write your book, we strongly advise using a mind map to get your thoughts out on paper. If you're not familiar with 'mind mapping' simply grab a blank piece of paper and write a working title in the centre of the page (you'll likely change this later once the content of the book becomes clearer), then from that centre working title, map out as many different points as you can which you think you'd like to cover in the book.

You can do several drafts of your mind map, so don't worry about it being perfect, but one of the key secrets is to start with the main working title and then select 10 main points you want to cover, which become your ten chapters, and then within each chapter, you want three smaller points which illustrate the main point you're making in each chapter.

Once you've mapped out the 10 major points you want to cover (don't worry about chapter titles yet – they'll come from the content as you write - just give them working titles for now), map out the three different points you want to cover in each chapter. This shouldn't take long at all, and if you've been thinking for a little while about writing a book, you'll find you move very quickly through this exercise.

Within literally 30-60 minutes, you'll not only have a broad outline for the book, but you'll also have a working title and chapter headings to reflect on, as well as the main points you're going to cover within each chapter. How cool is that? It's a lot quicker than most people think.

With this broad outline, another secret is to switch to a spreadsheet or table format on your computer and start expanding on each of the different sub points. Write quick notes on each one, bullet-pointing for efficiency. Don't worry about grammar or spelling or even sentence structure, just get the ideas down that you want to cover.

This is particularly useful if you also have quick stories you can share which help to go deeper on the concepts you're sharing, or will paint a vivid picture for your reader. Storytelling helps people to remember things more clearly than just plain text, so make sure you use them.

By now, you've got a broad outline of your book in mind map format, and you've built a list of content ideas for each chapter. How long has that taken you? Maybe 2-3 hours? You're cooking on gas!

Take Advantage Of Technology

For most people, the prospect of sitting down in front of a computer and writing for hours on end to create a book will seem incredibly daunting. This thought alone is what puts most people's dreams of becoming a published author firmly into a pair of 'concrete wellington boots' which get tossed overboard into the River Thames never to be seen ever again…

Don't let this thought overshadow you as there are far too many options available to you nowadays to make this dream a reality. Also, don't let the excuse that you're "too busy" get in the way either. Your published book has the potential to change the course of your personal and professional life forever.

As a quick aside, when we started the journey to become a published author and wrote the book 'As Safe As Houses' it was quite an intense process. To be honest, we paid several thousand pounds to learn this strategy which we're giving you for next to nothing, so please, do yourself a favour and take action on what we're sharing with you.

The quickest and easiest way to write your book is to start dictating it and not to worry too much about how the book will look or sound as you're just trying to get most of the ideas down on paper which can then be tied up during the editing process.

We suggest taking advantage of technology and using a dictation and transcription app on your phone or computer to help you get your book completed as quickly as possible (which is a process we've used extensively in the writing of this book).

Currently, we're using an app called 'Just Press Record' on our Mac laptop and the process is very simple. We have our notes in front of us, so we just press the record button and talk at our laptop for anywhere between 10-15 minutes at a time. Speaking is cool because the average talking speed is probably three times faster than your typing speed, so you can cover a lot of ground in a very short period of time.

This technology did not exist many years ago, so take advantage of it so you can produce your content in the shortest time possible. Another benefit of speaking is the tone of the book will be more conversational, rather than trying to sound like a professor of English! If you want people to consume your work, you need to meet them at their level, and most are far more comfortable with conversational tones, and written at a High School level of English. Otherwise, they'll get bored, or overwhelmed, and not bother reading it – that means you lose the opportunity to influence the reader to use your services.

Another secret is to do a test run of the first couple of chapters because unless you're used to dictating regularly, the whole process can feel a bit uncomfortable the first couple of times you do it. So, grab the first chapter of your book, speak at your computer at a reasonable pace and then move onto the second chapter to repeat the process.

Once you've done the first two, you'll hopefully feel less awkward and have the confidence which comes with at least making a start on an ambitious project, as that is one of the hardest things to do when it comes to doing anything new. There's a saying that suggests a project started is half-finished, and we think there's no truer saying when it comes to writing a book.

So now you've gone through the test of dictating a couple of chapters, go back and calmly and carefully dictate your first chapter again, taking the time to breathe and work through your book notes. As the transcriptions may be a little incorrect, its best to just do one chapter per recording as it breaks the workload nicely into sections. Then hit the transcribe button and cut and paste the completed text into a Word document you can edit to give you more of a formal structure.

Once you have this, it's just a case of sitting down and taking an hour or two every so often to edit each individual chapter. Invariably, more and more ideas will come to you which you can then incorporate into the book. Doing it a bit at a time will make the whole writing process so much easier.

If all this sounds like a little too much work, depending upon your resources, you could hire someone to ghost write your book for you, or you could dictate it and get a typist to type it for you. There's plenty of options, but they all require some investment of time or money (sometimes both).

Finally, don't get too carried away thinking your book has to be a thousand pages long. Just 100-150 pages is more than sufficient to concisely get your message across to your target audience and establish your authority, all presented in a quick & easy read designed to add value to your client.

Getting The Book Published

Never forget, the reason you're producing your book is as an instruction-getter, not to necessarily become a bestselling author. Do not lose sight of this as writing a book is a task that could go on for years if you let it. The point is to get it done as quickly and as efficiently as possible in the minimum amount of time, so it's done rather than perfect. You can always tweak it, or update it, or add more to it later, but you must get the first draft done asap.

It's helpful to adapt to the mantra; 'Done is better than perfect' and whilst the finished manuscript may not be 100% correct and a work of literary genius, the fact it's done, complete, and finished is far better than having a half-finished manuscript on your computer consuming data storage for millennia.

For the ambitious amongst you who feel you're going to be writing for days and weeks on end, you may be surprised to realise you can knock out a short, instruction winning book in a very short amount of time. The mere fact that you're handing your completed book to your prospect will likely wow them enough. Worry about updating it or polishing it later on.

When it comes to publishing, it's very difficult to beat Amazon in this arena. Amazon can get their books printed and published at costs substantially lower than most other self-publishing platforms. They've simply set themselves up to help self-publishers get to market as quickly and as cheaply as possible.

Before you go through the process of uploading it, you may want to have a book editor read the transcript to check it over for you, and a formatter to set it up in the exact templates which Amazon use to publish their books and eBooks. You can find people to do this for you, and ghost-writers if you choose to go down this route, on outsourcing sites like Fiverr. They're usually pretty cost effective for the burden of work they take off your shoulders, and it's another pair of eyes to review your work and get it to the final destination.

Finally, you'll also find book cover designers on sites like Fiverr who can help you with graphics and making the book look attractive, but again, don't go overboard and get too carried away with this as its possible to spend a fortune and not get the project finished.

You should also get a draft copy printed and review it before you finally sign it all off for public consumption. Be warned though; literally every author in the world reads their work after its printed and cringes a little – it's a totally normal reaction and you'll always think there's something that can be improved. Ignore that impulse and get it out to the world!

Becoming A Best Seller

Having looked into the mechanics of becoming a "Best-selling" author extensively, we're not fans of the whole process. The harsh truth is most people who advertise themselves as a bestselling author have quite literally paid their way to get this title.

The process typically involves selecting a niche category in which not many books sell, and using that category for the authors book, priming a group of would-be buyers who are interested in buying the book (namely friends and family), setting up a launch date, announcing the book launch, and encouraging all the friends to buy the book exactly on the launch hour, so it shoots up to the number one slot.

The moment the best-selling author spot is reached in that particular niche, the agency quickly takes a screenshot which is then used to promote the authors status as "bestseller". Even if ten seconds later the book loses the top spot, or in some cases doesn't sell more than 20 copies, the author can claim they're a best-seller forever. To us, this is inauthentic and it's certainly a far cry from being a bestselling author on the New York times bestsellers list, which some people often confuse this status with.

Whether or not you decide to go down this route with your own book is up to you, however it should not detract from getting it done and using it as a massive instruction winner for your business. The likelihood of your competition following suit is slim to none because most people don't want to do the work and would rather struggle being broke.

In fact, producing your own book as an instruction winner could be just another sign that they're going to continue to cut fees and overvalue as that's all they know. Don't follow suit. Do the opposite. Your work and the hidden secrets shared here will make you worth far more than your competition, and your prospects will know it.

So, JFDI – Just F*cking Do It!

As an aside, if you'd like some expert content to help fast track your success in getting your book published, just let us know. For a limited number of clients (to preserve its authenticity), we may be able to provide some killer content to help grow your business and show that you truly are the authority in your area.

Finally, for those of you who are interested in knowing the potential ramifications of becoming a published author, we encourage you to read Daniel Priestley's book, Key Person Of Influence.

If you want to know how you can really add value to your clients and your business, there's a ton of extra resources we can share with you on a call.

We just ask you to invest 30 minutes into a complimentary consultation, where we can help fast-track your success (with no hard sell whatsoever).

Here's the link to book your call:

http://www.wiggywam.co.uk/estateagentssecretscall

CHAPTER FIVE

THE HIDDEN SECRETS
BEHIND WIGGYWAM

Without this chapter just becoming a shameless plug for our property platform, we wanted to share some crucial information with you that we know is really going to help you rapidly implement everything we've been talking about in this book series so far, as well as what you'll cover by the end of this volume.

After all, without implementing what you've learnt, you're only getting a fraction of the value available.

Let's get the most obvious part out of the way first. A lot of people we talk to make the mistake of confusing WiggyWam with online portals such as Rightmove, Zoopla, or OnTheMarket. You're probably familiar with these portals because they're the ones sucking cash straight out of your wallet every single month (ha ha).

WiggyWam is worlds apart different because not only is the portal element a very small part of what we do, we've actually designed our whole business to serve two objectives:

1)   To help estate and letting agents win more instructions
2)   To help estate and letting agents to increase their fees

If you've learnt anything from these books so far, you can see we've gone above and beyond the call of duty by delivering on these two objectives. We've covered a ton of secret information, tips, and techniques to easily help you win more instructions and increase your fees to make your business more profitable.

But to us, it was vital we help you achieve this, without increasing your workload. We've all got too much to do and piling on another ton of work to your to-do list is not going to go down well with anyone. That's why we've designed our platform in a way that makes your operation more efficient and effective, so you can win more listings at greatly improved fees.

Here are some of the secret features we've built into the platform and how they help you and your business (and if you're not using them, you're missing out):

- **Priceless Learning Centre** – Quickly implement everything we've talked about in the Estate Agent's Secrets Trilogy using our innovative learning centre. Take advantage of the priceless knowledge and information we've already uploaded to the centre to help educate your clients, so they're more informed in their moving journey (saving you tons of time answering questions, whilst making your service incredibly valuable when you offer them access to this information as part of your fee). Quickly create unlimited online courses for your prospects nurturing journey (including paid and free options), with modules, lessons, tests, and certificates for ultimate professionalism. Create your own content or add video and audio files from sites like YouTube, Vimeo and Soundcloud etc. (you can even batch import your files for great efficiency). Educate yourself and your staff using our library of podcasts or training videos available immediately on demand, 24 hours a day, 7 days a week. The potential here is limitless.

- **Wonderful Workspaces** – Slash transaction times and countless phone calls or emails from clients using our innovative workspaces. They're automatically created when each property is first uploaded to the site – all you need to do is invite all parties to the deal so they can receive regular updates. The workspace tracks all milestones in the race to completion, so everyone knows what stage the deal is at, and the timeline let's people share documents, ask questions, and post the latest updates. You can even add your own workspaces for example when you're managing renovation projects for your clients (as we talk about later in this Volume), as another stream of income.

- **Cool Communication Through Instant Chat, Voice Call and Video Call** – Get ahead of the competition by using our instant communication tools. Save yourself a fortune in subscriptions to third party services and maintain the highest levels of privacy, all built into a secure, end-to-end encrypted system putting you instantly in contact with potential sellers in a couple of clicks. You can use these on your laptop, desktop, tablet, or smartphone, to communicate locally or internationally. Drop any file format into the chat box to quickly share with others and even set up group chat rooms for more private group discussions. We even installed an awesome translator into the system so you can text talk with anyone in their mother tongue and still get the message in English (or any language you prefer).

- **Magnificent Marketplace** – Use this for rapid success in your business networking and generating referrals. Quickly build the right power teams to repair and renovate client's properties so you can make a fortune. Find Joint Venture partners to do deals with and make even more money or find your next great hire using the jobs section. The power of this element of the platform is not to be underestimated.

- **Social Media Hacks** – Save time by managing multiple Social Media accounts, including Instagram, all in one secure place.

- **Promote Your Individual Or Company Profiles** – For you, your staff and your company, however you see fit. Show your prospects you can offer more of a personalised service, and let people get to know you, by sharing what's important to you.

- **Powerful Publishing** – Share articles of interest on your profile or create your own to show off your knowledge and bring potential clients into your world to win their instruction.

- **Create Super Surveys** – Don't guess, ask! Find out what the market needs, then provide the valuable solutions they'll happily pay you for.

- **MLS** – Make that cash register ring through using the MLS system build right into the platform.

- **Prolific Property Portal** – Maximum the exposure of your clients' homes using the in-built Property Portal. Add interactive virtual tours, floorplans, and as many listings as you like for a truly unlimited service (at no extra cost). People can share property details via social media, WhatsApp, and email to help increase exposure to more buyers. We even have the option of plugging you into 100's of additional sites to really get your client's properties out there (we're not precious – we just want to do the right job for our clients).

- **Exciting Events** – Run and manage any events you may want to put on such as open houses or landlord update seminars. You can even host virtual events and webinars right within the platform, so it's all in one secure place.

- **Fantastic Forums** – There's forums built right into the platform where you can get help for anything WiggyWam related, and also start new threads on discussions which matter most to you.

- **Censorship-Free** – We think this is vital in today's cancel culture. As long as you're not posting anything pornographic or which might endanger the life of another, we promise we won't ban you (that's reasonable, right)?

Expanding on the workspaces, let's say you're an estate agent and you've agreed a sale on a property. You can quickly invite the buyer, seller, both solicitors and the mortgage broker to join if you want to. All communication is then held within the workspace, so everybody is kept fully abreast with what's going on with the deal.

So, when you're chasing sales and speaking to lots of different people, sometimes sellers or buyers forget what you told them, but when you simply post the update in the workspace, it's there as a permanent record of progress for all to see. You can upload documents, attachments, and photos, (like a Facebook timeline), so everyone can see exactly what's going on and refresh their memory, without having to take up your valuable time with a wasted phone call or several emails back and forth.

There's also a task list which tracks progress, so as each time a task is completed, it's crossed off so everyone can see how far they've got to go before their deal is complete. This is invaluable to agents and their clients as moving home is so stressful and a lot of clients don't understand what goes on behind the scenes – the tracking tool helps focus their minds on what needs to be done before they make their move. This reduces the number of needless calls from anxious clients, or agents to solicitors chasing updates or wondering what the next step in the process is.

With the online learning centre, not only are you able to share your valuable knowledge and information, but you can also set up your own courses online. And by hosting the courses on WiggyWam, you can share them with your clients as free or paid-for options.

For example, let's say you set up a nurturing program where you share knowledge and information about what it's like to live in a particular area or what it's like to hire a removal company or how to hire a conveyancing solicitor. This educates people 24 hours a day, 7 days a week; a marketing system for your business which means you do the work once, and it pays for itself forever.

Can you see how tremendously valuable this is to your business? You could also do interviews with people for podcasts and host all this information in one place which people can easily see: far more powerful than any other property-related site in the world.

For agents reading this, who understand the secrets we've shared so far, will totally see why we built a dedicated learning section into the site for their clients who need to know more about what's involved in moving home.

When your prospect has a wealth of knowledge and information at their fingertips and you've taken the time to record some videos guiding them through what it is you do, they'll be truly grateful. As a client of WiggyWam, you can also share our knowledge and resources with your clients, helping you to stand out from the crowd (and drastically cutting down the amount of work you have to do). We've done most of the heavy lifting for you, so you don't have to.

For those who want to take things a step further, you can create all sorts of news articles and other additional resources which you can share with your target audience to really demonstrate your knowledge and expertise in one central place and use this platform to build your network and audience to become the go-to person in your area, locality, or even industry.

We've built the whole thing to put expert agents at the heart of the client's property journey. A key point of that is to empower you and your business by making you central to the whole deal and more visible as far as your prospects are concerned. Now think about how you're lost in a sea of obscurity with all the other agents on the 'property aggregator' sites, who put their business first...

Where would you rather be:

1. Lost in a sea of obscurity against every other agent online?

2. Have your business put front and centre in a way which naturally draws the right clients to you who will willingly pay you a handsome fee in exchange for your expertise?

Don't forget, you can also host all your vital resources on the platform for staff training too. When you're running a busy organisation and you want to outsource the way you do things, record a simple video explanation of what you're doing, upload it to a private part of your learning centre and invite all your staff to watch the training.

They can even interact with you and receive certificates once they've completed the training. The leverage you get in your business is huge - you only record the video information once but it's there forever. People who consume your videos or training courses will feel like they've been taken care of, and given a ton of value.

Finally, let's be perfectly frank about it: we want to work with you as a client.

No-one cares more about your business than you do, but we're a close second, so we want to see you succeed. It sounds corny, by your success is our success and if you're not successful, we have no business model worth talking about!

So, here's the deal, jump on a call with one of our team and invest 30 minutes seeing how we can help you quickly implement everything you've learnt so far. There's a ton of resources, knowledge, and expertise we couldn't include here that we'd love to share with you, so you can finally get the business you want and live the life you deserve.

Here's the link to book your free 30-minute executive briefing call (with no hard sell – just helpful guidance to get you to where you need to be):

http://www.wiggywam.co.uk/estateagentssecretscall

CHAPTER SIX

THE HIDDEN SECRETS TO GROWING YOUR LETTING AGENCY

What if there was a way to rapidly grow your letting agency, would you be interested in learning all about it? But you must be thinking, 'it's not like someone who knows all the hints, hacks, tips, and tricks is going to willingly share these with their potential competition, is it?' Well, luckily for you, after some behind-the-scenes' investigations with top performing companies, we're going to share them with you, right here!

You see, there are hidden secrets you can learn so you too can become the fastest growing letting agent in your area without endless prospecting, working all through the night, or spending a fortune on ads. We're excited to share this with you because to us, this is a complete no-brainer strategy that any forward-thinking letting agent can use to rapidly grow their business. Or if you're an estate agent looking to bolt on a lettings side to your business, this is absolutely what you should be doing to generate tons more revenue and establish yourself very quickly in the marketplace.

What we're about to share will literally blow your mind but you might be a little confused as to how you can put it into practice. Don't worry, we're not going to leave you in the lurch! We've got a ton of invaluable resources to support you on your journey. We've put a ton of time, effort, money, and years of expertise into developing this framework which will fast track you to roll out the ideas discussed here as a new service for your prospective clients. So, grab yourself a pad and a pen to take some notes as we go through this exciting journey together.

(It might not be a bad idea to buy a money counter too…).

Before we get into this, we need to make a quick disclaimer, because unfortunately, we're moving more and more towards a litigious society. We're showing you what has worked for some people we know personally in their business, but importantly, we're not promising a get-rich-quick-scheme, nor do we have any control over the time and effort you dedicate to implementing these strategies, nor the results you'll achieve. So, keep an open mind when reading – you'll need to invest some serious efforts if you want to succeed with these secret strategies, and you can't expect the "magic business fairies" to come along and start generating more income for you! That's not what this is all about, okay?

Finally, we need to point out that we're not financial advisors, nor are we providing any regulated financial, or legal advice in any way. If you're in any doubt whatsoever, then you should always seek professional advice.

A Shortcut For You And Your Business

Lately, we've seen a lot of comments on social media asking; "How do I win more landlords?" Or "How do I expand my business?" Or "I'm a new letting agent starting up and don't know where to find those elusive landlords." Or "I've got an existing portfolio of clients, but I can't seem to get up to the next level". There seems to be a lot of frustration around winning new business.

We'll expose the real secrets for you here to drive your business forward, by getting landlords on board in such a way that they'll stay with you long term. So, let's take you from a place of frustration, to being the agent who wins more and more business by generating revenue from areas you're currently overlooking. It's money you may not even realize you're leaving on the table (or is going straight into your competitor's pockets – and we definitely don't want that – do we…?).

Some Background

Over the last decade, we've been fortunate to interview literally hundreds of estate and letting agents up and down the country as we trained new and experienced property investors alike. What was surprising, was in every town or area of a city that we went to, out of all available options, there was always one estate or letting agent that stood out head and shoulders above everybody else. It was a pattern we noticed coming up time and time again.

Sometimes it would be a corporate agent and sometimes a self-employed small business owner, but either way, they were the ones who talked our language and so were the agents of choice to do business with. We also noticed a huge chasm between most estate and letting agents and their attitude towards property investors and landlords. Not only were those agents lacking the specialist knowledge to win our confidence, but some were also downright hostile towards us when we mentioned we were property investors. As a result, there was never a chance of them winning our business. The worst even suggested they needed brown paper envelopes filled with cash in order to supply us with deals…

It's up to you how you want to run your business, but what we can share with you is simply not knowing these secrets we're about to share with you, a lot of agents are costing themselves literally tens of thousands in lost revenue – money that would make a huge difference to the quality of their life and business.

So, what did the best agents do? The best of the best agents, all had five things in common:

1.   They were Proactive

Being proactive demonstrates great qualities about you and your business. One example is where a letting agent actively puts together a landlord pack for new & existing clients looking to buy in their area. Any agent could easily put such a pack together, provided free of charge, which demonstrates your knowledge about which areas of town are the best to invest in, and which are best avoided. You can also explain which types of property are in high demand.

After you've given this helpful information, give your prospect an idea of the services you provide to look after their investment for them. Share stories about how you went above and beyond the call of duty with your clients to help them out. If you and your staff members also invest, let your clients know.

Perhaps with a little thought, you can come up with other ideas of what to include which adds massive value, yet which cost little to implement. Is all this effort worth it, you may ask? Well let's ask another question – how many of your current competitors are doing something like this? In our experience, very few. So, do you think you'll stand out against the competition if you're the only one offering a brand package of high-quality information to a prospect? The answer will undoubtedly be, yes! And if you've been following along with the contents of these books, you'll know it makes sense to do so.

This serves another purpose too; it allows less experienced staff to learn from your expertise, thus increasing the level of service offered, even if they can't relay it to the investor themselves. Have some fun with this and see what you can come up with.

It could be a USB with some informative videos on it, (or even better, inviting them to watch your videos on your WiggyWam private learning centre), or it could be a deal-analysis service where you would offer to price up the refurbishment works, manage the refurbishment and sell or let the property at the end of it. For a fee of course!

You might find this strategy alone will bring you more work than you can handle – read on to find out more.

2.   They Knew Their Area Better Than Anyone Else

There's a saying in the investment world which is; 'You don't know what you don't know'. This seems self-explanatory, but it's also true that what you don't know can get you hurt or into a lot of trouble. Similarly, your client doesn't know what you know, so you must share your knowledge so they can make an informed choice on whether or not to work with you.

This is one of the reasons why we feel the larger corporate agents have struggled so much recently because it simply comes down to this; trying to use the McDonald's approach (hiring the youngest and cheapest staff and training them to run systems), in agency doesn't work in our humble opinion.

If you're looking to sell your £500,000 home, you don't want to speak to a youngster who has no experience in buying and selling homes. You want to deal with people who know what they are talking about and have expertise. Yes, everyone has to learn and not all youngsters are the same, but you can't expect someone to do business with you and your agency, especially <u>trusting you with the most expensive asset they own</u>, if you and your staff haven't shown them that you know what you're talking about.

One pet peeve to mention here was asking agents which areas we should or should not invest in and the agent then refusing to comment. We went into their office to seek their expertise and were given a weak answer as to why they couldn't provide it. Subsequently, there was never any possibility they would win our business.

3. They Were Investors Themselves

When an agent told us they were investors themselves, it was music to our ears. There's a world of difference between agents who manage properties for others, and those who own investment property themselves.

You understand the personal impact of void periods. You understand why it's essential to get maintenance and repair work done as economically as possible (notice we didn't say 'as cheaply' as possible). You understand how to make sure the tenant pays their rent on time and how to swiftly remove them from the property if they don't. You understand, through personal experience that a landlord's property isn't just a number on the whiteboard in the office, it can be their livelihood which can eat them alive if it's not managed properly.

When agents demonstrate their hands-on expertise, investors can have a very different conversation with them and trust between both parties is automatic. So, if you're not an investor already, don't worry because what we're going to show you all the information you need to sound like an expert (and also start building your own portfolio on the side if you want to).

4. They Listened Carefully To Their Clients And Their Requirements

This might sound obvious, but it's amazing how many agents get this wrong. It's vital to listen carefully to what your potential client is saying and respond to what they're asking for, not what you think they're asking for. If there's any doubt at all, simply ask qualifying questions to drill down to get certainty, or to help your client to shift their mindset.

Oftentimes, confusion in a conversation comes from the agent lacking the knowledge they should have to engage at a deeper level. When you think you know how something works, such as property investment, it can be very difficult to consider a different view. It's called cognitive dissonance. And it can wreak havoc on your ability to build a relationship with an investor.

The reason we say this is because we've had countless conversations with agents where there was complete misalignment between what we said we wanted, and what the agent understood about our needs.

As an example, let's say we knew from our research that a two-bedroom terraced property around £90,000 would work best for our investment strategy. Yet when we shared this with agents, they started trying to sell us 3-bedroom semi's at £120,000! Can you see how frustrating that would be? It's akin to going to buy a motorbike and the salesman trying to sell you a car!

It's perfectly acceptable to say that you don't have anything suitable, but you'll keep in contact with them should anything come up. But when you make that promise, make sure you do it and only send relevant properties to them. All too often we see agents take the 'scattergun' approach of sending lots of properties to potential investors which wastes a lot of time for all parties. It may work for buyers of homes to live in, but investors are far more specific in what they're looking for.

5. They Kept Their Commitments

By far, this was the biggest test we used to see if an agent was worth working with. After we'd called in to visit them and engaged in a conversation, there were invariably some action points which came out of the conversation that the agent had agreed to take on. They always promised they would "get back to us".

Yet, it was amazing how many times they failed to do so. It would not be uncommon when visiting an area to hit an 80-90% strike rate of agents failing to make the grade by not getting back to their potential investor client. This was even more embarrassing for the agent when the investor had 5-10 properties they were self-managing but who couldn't pass them over to a letting agent because they didn't keep their commitments.

The ones who won the business were sometimes the only agent to get back to us! So, if you want to stand the best chance of winning business from portfolio landlords and investor clients who will continually buy more properties and put them with you for management, <u>get back to people when you say you will.</u>

Why Are We Sharing These Hidden Secrets With You?

Well, quite honestly, we're very concerned about the way the economy is going and the future of the UK property industry. We see some big problems on the horizon that almost no-one is talking about, and which could literally put a lot of businesses on life support, or close them for good. We're very concerned about the way things are shaping up for everybody, particular after the pandemic we've recently experienced.

Sure, the market has bounced back hard after the first lockdown, but (at the time of writing), there are already signs the market is slowing down, prices are reducing, and the lack of stock is killing some agents.

Whilst we've enjoyed a very good market, what happens if, as, and when, we hit the next recession because it can't go on indefinitely, right? So, when we hit the next recession (or even a depression, which is what some top economists have warned about), how does this impact your business? We're not trying to be Doom and Gloom - we're trying to provide a dose of reality so you can be ahead of the game when the adverse economy comes, which might otherwise wipe out your business.

For those of you that were in the agency game in 2008 (during the credit crunch), it was almost as if someone came into your office and unplugged the phones! They stopped ringing literally overnight. And because not many people were able to get mortgages, properties were selling up to 50% less than their market value a year before.

We honestly feel that's one of the problems that could be on the horizon again. What happens if we have another credit crunch because of the pandemic? What happens if there's massive inflation or interest rates rise (as is already happening)? What impact could this make to people's finances or ability to afford to keep their properties (or your own)? On the flip side, we also believe there will always be massive opportunities for those people who take the right actions and create their own destiny.

For those readers with a little bit more experience in the world, you'll know as sure as night follows day that after a boom, usually follows a recession. And after a recession usually follows a boom. We're about overdue now for a recession although there's many people who don't agree with us on that, and they think the current boom is going to last forever, (which is a very typical thought pattern in a boom period).

Warren Buffett says it best: "Be fearful when others are greedy and greedy when others are fearful." Wise words from one of the richest men on the planet.

Who Does This Work For?

The priceless secrets we're sharing here work for any agent who wants to start or grow their lettings business and who are determined to take action to not only learn this information, but to implement it. It also works if you who want to avoid losing landlords to your competition by handcuffing them to your business, so they don't go anywhere else.

Finally, for those agents who want to make maximum profit from every deal that comes across their desk, you'll kick yourself when you realise exactly how much money has slipped through your fingers over the years.

But first, let's look at some fatal mistakes letting agents make, so you can avoid them. Once you understand these fatal mistakes, you'll realise what you need to do, and what services you can offer your clients, to make you an indispensable asset to their business.

You'll be able to offer significant value which nobody else in the marketplace is offering because they're all doing the same as one another. Trust us; we've interviewed hundreds of agents up and down the country and we've yet to see 1 in 100 talk about the secrets we're disclosing here. So read on to find out more.

Fatal Mistake Number One - You don't talk your target market's language.

This is one of the most misunderstood things we try to convey to agents because they think they understand landlords and property investors. For the most part, when agents talk to what we call an amateur landlord, (somebody who owns a single property, usually their former home, and decides to rent it out), they're just renting out the property to cover the mortgage whilst you're managing it for them.

Unfortunately, most agents only have the limited knowledge to deal with such scenarios and as such, don't know how to really talk to professional landlords, who could bring them 5, 10, 15, or 20 properties in one hit, and who will buy at least 1-2 properties a year to help grow your business.

Here's what used to happen frequently during mentorships with investors when we went into an estate or letting agent's office: we'd say something like, "Hi, How are you? We're Professional Property Investors and we're in the area looking for deals." We weren't talking a great game; we were introducing ourselves and depending upon what feedback we got from the agent would instantly determine whether or not we would feel comfortable enough to give them our business.

We appreciate agents get bombarded with people talking a great game about being a landlord or property investor. However, if your response to such enquiries is to come across as naïve, uninterested, or not knowing what you should know as an agent, then most investors or professional landlords just aren't going to do business with you. What's the saying; 'you never get a second chance to make a great first impression?' That's something you need to have at the forefront of your mind when engaging with investors as they're just too profitable to ignore.

Another problem we experienced is agents employing younger staff in their office who had no experience in buying, selling, or renting properties themselves. They were good at going through the motions but didn't fully understand what's involved. So, when experienced investors or landlords go into an agent's office and they're faced with somebody in their late teens or early 20's, who's not talking the same language, there's going to be a huge gap in the conversation and a lack of faith. Unfortunately, this happened so many times we cannot even begin to calculate the cost of lost business for these agents.

The Biggest Myth Of Property Investment

A lot of agents mistakenly think property investors buy for capital appreciation. That's got to be the biggest myth in the entire industry. Now, if you're a Russian oligarch, and you've got loads of money (millions), to buy up terraced houses for cash and rent them out then, this might not apply to you. But for the 99.9% of other investors in the marketplace who don't have that sort of money to throw around, they may mistakenly buy for capital appreciation but when the market turns south, they quickly realise they got it wrong.

We cannot emphasize this enough - buying for capital appreciation alone is not how you make money in property. And if you mistakenly suggest to an investor that it is, you're never going to get their business.

For example, some people, have always bought in London because the common misconception is London always goes up in value, right? It's always going up so people will always make money. Yet it's simply not true. Look at the impact of the Grenfell Tower fire and the pandemic on demand and values in London recently. Some people are completely unable to sell their flats because of cladding claim issues, so what are those properties worth now?

Knowing The Numbers

Further, over 90% of agents, don't understand the numbers when it comes to property investment. Now, you might think, 'what the hell are these guys at WiggyWam talking about?' Well, bear with us and we'll reveal all. Be aware, there's a completely different mindset when talking about cashflow on investment property, versus capital growth, versus yield, (the latter is what a lot of agents talk about).

Yield, to be quite honest, is a fallacy. Again, a very bold statement to make and you're probably sitting there in your seat, huffing, and puffing and saying to yourself, 'This guy doesn't have a clue what he's talking about!' But trust us, when you see all this begin to unfold, it will start to make a lot more sense and ultimately help you to become a lot more profitable. After all, if you were doing something that was costing you a lot of business, wouldn't you rather know about it so you could put it right, even if it conflicted with some of your core beliefs?

What Is Cashflow?

So, let's talk about the numbers and how we view property investment through the eyes of a professional investor. We want to know that the deal cashflows.

What does cashflow mean?

At the end of every month, does the deal put more money into our pocket after all the bills are paid? That's what we want to achieve.

A lot of investors can't buy properties as outright cash purchases. Whilst they may say they're cash buyers, at some point they will likely put a mortgage on the property. So, what we need to know is, once the mortgage and all the other expenses are paid, does the deal still put money in our pocket?

This principle alone is what drives the offers investors make when buying a property and is usually a cause of frustration for the agents when their offer comes in low.

But before you dismiss investors as total cheapskates, let's cover the cashflow calculation, so you can understand this principle in greater detail.

With property investing, each one is viewed as a standalone unit. Even though an investor might have 10 or 20 other units, each individual property must stand on its own two feet. Investors look at the rental income, then make allowances for the following deductions: the mortgage, the management costs, and M.O.E.

What is M.O.E., you ask? It stands for Monthly Operating Expenses. There are other things investors need to consider which most people overlook, such as any repairs required to keep the property habitable. Just as a taxi driver must cover the costs of fuel and repairs to his car, an investor has to cover the costs of maintenance and periodic inspections if their business is to work properly.

The typical mindset of most amateurs is to buy a property to rent out, pay their mortgage each month and self-manage it. They think that's it. But they're not factoring in any repairs or maintenance. They ought to account for the fact that the boiler always seems to blow up on December 24th, or the property may need some form of emergency repair, or that the roof might need replacing sometime in the future.

This is where M.O.E. comes into play and we're yet to see a letting agent explain this to us in detail.

The Cashflow Calculation

As professional property investors, we look at the rent coming in, (in this example, we're going to use £600pcm), then we have to deduct the costs of the mortgage (say £350pcm), the management costs (we'll use 10% of the rent although some of you may charge more), and finally the Monthly Operating Expenses factored in at another 10%.

What savvy investors do is, set aside £60 into a separate bank account every single month to cover such things as repairs, maintenance, and void periods. At the end of the calculation, we aim to end up with a profit, which in the below example, is £130 per month. This doesn't sound like earth shattering numbers, we appreciate, but there's a reason why which we'll cover later.

Rental Income:	£600pcm
Mortgage:	£350pcm
Management Fee @10% of rent:	£60pcm
MOE @ 10% of rent:	£60pcm
Monthly Profit:	£130pcm

This is a fairly simple calculation, but we guarantee if we ask most letting agents if they know what a cashflow calculation is, they'll say no. Professional property investors run each property as a business and we stress this point to you, particularly if you want to win over established investors and portfolio landlords.

Knowing this, it's something you could offer as a service to your existing and future clients as part of a portfolio health-check. It's not that complicated to do, but it offers a great rapport building insight as to whether their property is cash flowing, and if not, they have the opportunity to do something about it – like selling it through your agency… ;-)

What most "amateur investors" do, is to buy a property because they fall in love with it, such as a new build off-plan flat. They're popular because investors are told they'll make loads of money in the future because not only are they buying it at a bargain price because of a heavy discount for buying now, property prices are going up, so by the time the building is complete and the flat is ready to market, it's going to be worth at least 20% more! Who in their right minds would want to pass on such a great deal?!

Unfortunately, this is marketing hype by the agent selling it on behalf of the builders, and fundamentally it doesn't work. What happens is most amateur investors end up in a situation where their mortgage cost alone is equal to, or greater than, the rent, or when you factor in the other costs we've just outlined, they end up making a loss.

Now, the amateurs will say, "well, I'm only paying the mortgage and I'm managing it myself, so I don't really have to worry about that and it's a new property, so I don't really need to consider the Monthly Operating Expenses so I'm not really losing that much money. I'm only losing £50-£100 a month, which is fine because it's an investment and it's my pension..." It's the same old rhetoric we've heard a million times! There's an emotional attachment which leads to trying to justify a loss-making property.

Now, if you're in business but you're making a loss on every property you buy, that's not good logic, is it? But sometimes amateurs adopt this backwards approach to end up compounding their losses, usually because of poor advice dispensed by people who should know better. They start out with one or two properties and if they're earning good money from their job or business, they'll buy a few more "investments". The costs continue to escalate and suddenly, they're losing £1,800 a month or more over 10 properties.

Again, this might not sound like a lot and people pass it off by thinking, "Oh, it's fine, the cost is manageable, and they're all going up in value at 10% a year, so I'm already making a killing." But does the property market really go up every year? Realistically, we know the answer is absolutely not! In 2008/2009, the property market dropped by around 25-30 %, which is a big loss to take on, especially if you need to sell because you ran into cashflow difficulties.

The amateur investor bought based on marketing hype and hasn't looked at the realistic values for their proposed purchase. So, they sign up to a mortgage deal based on an inflated market value, and an inflated rent (figures are usually provided by the builder or the agent acting on their behalf).

And here's where they kick themselves in the pants and don't even realise it…

When the building is complete, there's a ton of similar properties all coming to the market at the same time. The previously quoted high rental figures are a work of fiction and aren't achievable because prospective tenants for this type of property now have an overwhelming number of options to choose from. Inevitably, prices are then lowered to stimulate tenant demand.

When they realise they're faced with losing money, amateur investors then think, 'no problem, I'll simply sell the property and make some easy money because it's increased in value since I put my initial deposit down.' Yet, how many other people, faced with the similar situation of not being able to find a tenant to cover their costs, simply decide to sell at the same time? And with a glut of similar properties coming to the market all at once, are the high prices they expect to receive achievable?

But here's the hidden secret that destroys most investors who buy this type of property: once one property in the block sells for a much lower price because someone is desperate and needs to get out, it becomes a comparable which mortgage valuation surveyors consider for every other sale in the block. We've seen tons of examples where innocent amateur investors have lost tens, if not hundreds, of thousands of pounds because they didn't know what they were doing and relied upon poor quality 'advice' from people who don't know much better.

The fact is, we've seen many other examples where this has gone badly wrong for such investors, and we've had to work extremely hard to try and dig them out of a big financial hole. We met a couple of business partners in the Northeast of England, who had a really successful business which produced a load of cash. They took the amateur investor model of losing money and ended up buying over 300 properties! Most people would think 300 properties is amazing and they're set for life, but, with that sort of volume and losing, £50-£100+ per month, per property, it soon starts to add up. When the business starts to fail, they're faced with losing literally everything. They said, "the moment interest rates rise, by just 1%, we lose the portfolio, we lose the business, and we also lose our homes." To us, that's just too much of a worrying situation to be in.

We also knew of an Italian investor who was losing over €30,000 **a month** because he did not know what he was doing. Now, you might think we're exaggerating, but we can tell you hand-on-heart these sorts of things are going on all over the U.K. right now and it happens because people don't know any better. Now you do because you've been shown what investors should be doing when buying properties as standalone units. And they must be cashflow positive (i.e., producing a profit each month after all the bills are paid).

As an aside, if you do know people who are faced with a situation where they are losing money or faced with taking a financial loss on a property, get in touch with us straight away, so we can help find a solution. Do not leave it too long as the impacts of such situations can literally eat people alive financially. Send an email to HappyToHelp@WiggyWam.co.uk briefly outlining the situation and we'll see what we can do to help.

Now, what your clients should do, (or you could on their behalf by selling this as a service), is stress-testing their current portfolio. You've got the template for the cashflow calculation, and you'll know what rent is coming in because you're either the managing agent for the property, or you know the area well enough to know what it will fetch on the open market. You may not know what their current mortgage payment is, but you could ask the client for the amount of their mortgage and interest rate to work out the monthly payment (or use the figure on their bank statement each month).

One top secret tip is, we always recommend stress-testing deals by factoring in mortgage interest at a base rate of 6%. That's **base** rate, not the current actual interest rate. When stress-testing deals at 6% base rate, does it still cashflow or does it start to hurt the investor financially? When deals aren't working, then the simplest thing to do is to sell them or consider a higher and better use, such a turning them into serviced accommodation or a HMO.

The current market might be the best time for your clients who have these types of properties that aren't cashflowing, and who could be in danger of being financially crippled in the future, to get rid of them now. What the market's going to be like in six months' time, is anybody's guess; it could be on its knees or might have dropped 20%, so the best time to act is always now.

Ideally, you should be including M.O.E. at 10% as a minimum, or maybe even 15-20%, depending on the property (especially if it's a HMO, where you should use 20%). Then, include the management charge of 10% (or more) per month. This will really help your clients understand where they are at and to help them guard against any future problems that might crop up.

Calculating Mortgage Costs

One of the most frequent questions people ask is, "How do we calculate the mortgage costs?" Simply take the mortgage amount (in this example, we'll use £75,000), multiply it by the mortgage interest rate (say 6% or 0.06), which will give you the annual amount of interest, then divide that figure by 12 to give you the monthly amount.

For example:

£75,000 x 6% (or 0.06) = £4,500 annual interest.

$$\frac{£4,500}{12} = £375\text{pcm mortgage payment}$$

It's worth mentioning that most investors will use interest only mortgages for two reasons. First, they want their monthly payments to be as low as possible. Second, they're banking on the property value increasing substantially, so their debt-to-equity ratio falls substantially over time.

Your client should know the exact monthly payment because it'll be on their bank statement, but if you want to stress-test it, then we recommend you do the above simple calculation factoring in a base rate of 6%. Take the current percentage interest they're paying, deduct the current base rate from it, and then add 6% to it.

For example, if they're paying 2.9% and base rate is 0.5%, we deduct 0.5 from 2.9 to give 2.4%, then add 6% to it to give 8.9% as our stress-test mortgage interest rate. If the property doesn't cashflow at this new level, it might be time for your client to consider selling.

Now, it's important to say, a lot of your clients will be emotionally attached to their properties, and so won't want to let them go. Yet, that emotional attachment might pose a problem for them, either now or in the future. All you can do is offer the best advice you can to your client.

When you plant the seed in people's minds, and they start thinking, "Actually, if base rate goes up to 4%, this deal starts to lose money, and at 6%, its going to cost me, £200, £300, or more per month." So, you might find in two or three-month's time, they come back to you and decide to sell the property. That means more fees, and a good feeling knowing you've protected them from possible future financial hardships. Plus, they may even choose to buy one or two more properties from you that do work, and keep them with you for management, so this is a total no-brainer strategy.

What Most Agents And Mortgage Brokers Don't Know

Some of you reading this may get a little offended by what follows, but we're going to be brutally honest with you and share what you need to know, if you're going to have any chance of growing your business by targeting the investor and landlord market. A lot of agents talk about yield, and mistakenly say, 'landlords are looking for 6% yield on a deal' because it's very fashionable, and its how commercial properties are sold based on a percentage yield.

Yield is calculated by taking the monthly rent and multiplying it by 12 to give the annual income from that property. It's a bit like saying, "if I had £100,000 cash in the bank, and I was getting 6% interest (£6,000 a year), that's a 6%

yield." It's the same principle but we take that cash out of the bank and buy a property with it worth £100,000 which generates £6,000 a year gross rent.

It's completely fallacious to say this though, because as you now know it doesn't reflect the repairs, maintenance, upkeep, or refurbishment of the property which reduces the effective yield straight away (which doesn't happen with commercial properties let on FRI leases). We said before, a lot of clients won't be buying outright cash, so when you talk about yield to any professional investor, they immediately think you don't know what you're talking about.

When we used to speak on behalf of Robert Kiyosaki, Robbie Fowler, & Martin Roberts doing property investment seminars, we would talk to anywhere between 20-100+ people every weekend, and 99% of the people in the room did not know the simple concepts presented here. Over the course of three days, we'd show them what they needed to know, and for anyone who had already bought "investment property", we pulled apart their deals which invariably showed them that they didn't work. We also gave them an action plan on what to do. So, with the secret knowledge presented here, you can educate people and become the go-to agent in your area, as most others won't even know this basic information.

We talked about portfolio reviews earlier, particularly for those stubborn self-managing landlords who you've been trying to win over for some time now. You can offer them something which nobody else can. Tell them you'll do a free portfolio review, look at their current properties and see if they cashflow. Stress-test them to see if they really work and when they're impressed with your knowledge, you can take over the management of their properties. Offer the valuable service first, and then talk about them listing the property with you _after_ you've demonstrated your expertise (which they won't find anywhere else).

Finally, we should point out that if you work with a mortgage broker and you share the information we've shared so far, be very careful they don't try and talk you out of implementing it, or they laugh about interest rates rising etc. The fact is, nobody knows what the future may hold, so it's best to operate from a place of caution, rather than your clients' optimism putting them in a financial stranglehold in the future.

Fatal Mistake Number Two - Advising investors to pay retail, rather than wholesale.

Again, this is something which might ruffle a few feathers, so we make no apologies for it because it's essential to understand if you're going to get your lettings business running right for you. If you're not already investing in property, once you get over your initial scepticism of this comment, you'll see the potential this has.

The **single biggest mistake** we see investors make, because of poor quality advice given by others, is they fail to negotiate (well enough), on the properties they buy. Amateur investors always pay the 'retail' price whereas professional proper investors pay 'wholesale'. There's a massive difference between the two which means the professional pays as much as 50% less than the amateur.

The golden rule of property investment taught to us by Robert Kiyosaki is this; **you make your money when you buy,** yet most people think they make money when they sell because they make a profit <u>after</u> the property goes up in value. When a professional investor buys a property, they want to achieve a discount on its market value, at least equal to the deposit they would otherwise have to put into the deal, **plus** any refurbishment costs, **and** the costs of acquiring it in the first place. If you're not sure what we mean, reread this paragraph several times until the penny drops.

Now some of you are sitting there thinking, 'okay, that sounds like a lot of money' and sometimes it is. Sometimes that might be 30%+ discount to the market value of the property, so the natural response is, "there's no way you can buy properties, 20-30%, below market value!" But you absolutely can.

However, for context, what the amateurs do is this: let's say the market value for the property is £100,000, they pay £100,000 cash, or they might get a small mortgage. If they do get a buy to let mortgage, it's usually for 75%, and they put down a 25% deposit.

They then have £6,500+ worth of costs for the refurbishment and similar costs to legally buy it. They end up spending a total of £113,000 for a property that's still only worth £100,000! Does that make good business sense…? The answer is simply no.

They pay 13%+ above market value for the property which is an issue when it comes to trying to build a portfolio of investment properties because they end up over-capitalising each purchase. They put too much money into an asset (which isn't actually an asset because it doesn't cashflow – it takes money out of their pocket and hence is a liability). They reason the cost of refurbishment and purchase are just a cost of doing business and now at least they own a property, so they can tell all their mates when they go down the pub! And, you know, it's their pension, so it doesn't really matter that its losing money… because everybody else has lost a fortune on their pension recently anyway, and at least their money is in bricks and mortar which always goes up!

Ideally, when you're buying a property for investment, you want to know you can sell it the same day (or a few weeks later), for at least the price you paid for it. You can see from the numbers above that the amateur investors can't. Who's going to pay 13+% above market value for a property? So they're in a loss-making position from day one.

Worse, they have to wait a long time for the market to go up by 13+% just to get to break-even (without factoring in the costs to sell it)!

Yet, when you buy at a discount, you build a lot of security into your business. But, a lot of agents don't like investors trying to buy at a discount and it gets their backs up. There's a clash between the investors and the agents because they say, "I'm not going to put that offer to my client because it's 25% below what it's on the market for!" The investor replies, "Yes, because that's what works for me." The estate agent then says, "Oh no, I valued the property and that's what it's worth! Don't embarrass me in front of my client!"

Unfortunately for the agent, by taking an abrupt approach to the investor, they never get the opportunity to win their business. You've got to understand, to the property investor guys & girls, it is literally just a game, so roll with it. Have some fun with it and see what you can learn from the investor rather than being offended by their audacity to make such an offer! After all, doesn't it make total sense to work with them, lock them into your business and make money off them forever? Isn't this one of the best strategies you can employ?

Where Can You Find Deals?

People invariably ask where can you get property deals from if you can't buy them from estate agents? Well, there's many ways to buy properties that aren't via an estate agent. Look at auction purchases, buying via eBay, ask neighbours and people who live in the area if there might be a place they know that's coming up for sale. There's a whole bunch of creative ways to find deals you can use when you know how.

The good news for you reading this is you're already an estate or letting agent, so you have access to a whole bunch of clients who may have properties they're looking to sell quickly for whatever reason. All it needs is a little client contact and nurturing to flush out potential deals. You can also consider placing adverts in the local paper which are separate from your usual agency adverts, looking to find people who want to sell their property quickly. For ideas, pick up a copy of your local paper and look in the classified – there's bound to be some people advertising who want to buy investment property.

Negotiating The Deal

A lot of people get scared when it comes to negotiating a property deal, especially when they're not very good at negotiating, or when they feel their offer is too low that its embarrassing to put forward. Sometimes, even though agents are used to dealing with properties and offers day in and day out, the investment market can make them feel uncomfortable.

One of the reasons for this is they somehow feel that they're taking advantage of someone by making a lower than market value offer for the property. What they fail to understand is that many people who want to sell a property quickly, and therefore will accept a lower offer for a cash purchase, are doing so because a) their current financial position is very stressful and dictates the need to generate some quick cash or b) the property has become a millstone around their neck, and they just want rid of it.

For anyone who has not been in a position where they desperately need cash to fix a problem, you'll never quite understand why someone would choose to take a lesser offer for their property. In their minds, the seller is "losing" £20,000 or £30,000. Yet property is illiquid, and it can take many months to realise a gain through traditional means of selling. So, if someone comes along and can fix their financial problem within a month by buying it for cash, which could save the seller from losing £50-100,000, then they're winning, not losing.

You're probably never going to get to understand the full extent of someone's personal financial situation, but when they're selling their property for less than you might achieve on the open market, there's usually a good reason for it. And you may be doing them a huge favour when you're the one buying it, or facilitating the deal, rather than letting them be at the mercy of some 'investor' who has less morals than Tony Blair!

In any event, let's get you out of your comfort zone and help you practice your negotiation skills by playing a special little game. It's a secret game which we had the most fun with when it came to training new investors in the art of negotiation.

The objective of the game is to practice this in your day-to-day life by going out into the Big Wide World and getting something for free.

Now that doesn't involve theft, okay!

It doesn't involve stealing the charity box from the local shop, that's not what we're talking about here! Hone your negotiating skills by getting something for free, that has genuine value. It might be a free coffee, it might be a newspaper, it might be a packet of biscuits or something else; maybe it low in monetary value, but it should still give you the confidence to go out there, negotiate with people, and have some fun doing it.

You might think, "Why would I want to do this? Why don't I just pay for it because it's only a couple of quid?" The point is, it's getting over the fear of what other people might think of you and getting over your inherent fear of rejection.

Let's give you an example. We recently went to Costa Coffee and were chatting to the girl making the drink. We picked up a packet of biscuits and said, "Can we have these for free, please?" She looked confused, as much as to say, 'what are you talking about?' before responding with a smile and saying, "you can have it but you've got to pay for it!" We said with a smile, "Well look, there's a broken biscuit in here - of course you know you can't sell it now it's broken, can you?"

We were being cheeky and having a bit of fun. Of course, she might be thinking, 'okay, he's a bit of a weirdo,' but who cares? We then said, "I'm sorry, I'm just having a bit of fun with you! But if you've got anything for free, great, I'll take it right now!"

Anyway, we finished up, grabbed our coffee, high five'd the girl behind the counter and thanked her for being awesome, as we turned to walk away, she said, "Oh, excuse me…you can have these…" as she handed over the packet of biscuits with a big smile!

Now, it's not much, but the uplifting feeling you get from these little wins is enough to help you practice your negotiation skills and overcome any fear or embarrassment of what other people might think, especially innocent bystanders! So, go and have some fun with this game as we're sure you'll enjoy it.

Being Equitable

The reason why most people don't like the idea of buying a property at a discount is because of the fear they're ripping someone off and they'll get tarred with the same brush as a lot of rogue investors out there who are not particularly nice people. They're the type who try and shaft others when they realize they're in a difficult personal or financial situation, and they purposely lowball the offer to screw the seller down as much as possible, by holding them over the hot coals until they've got the price they want.

We want to say to you, when you're trying to buy property at a discount, you've got to act fast, be fair, and be Equitable.

For those of you who don't know what Equitable means, there's actually two branches of law in the UK; there's legal and legislation which is the law, and then there's Equity, which is more concerned with the 'moral code' of law. In Equity, a judge will look at the circumstances around why the issue has ended up in court and will look at it through the eyes of Equity to determine if the law, which is written in black and white and leaves little room for manoeuvre, is Equitable pertaining to that particular situation.

As an example, say somebody was caught speeding on the motorway, doing 80 miles an hour, when they should only be doing 70. The law will say, that's an offence punishable by a fine and three points on their driving licence. Whereas Equity might look at it and say, well, the lady was rushing her husband to hospital because his appendix burst and they had to get there quickly, so should there be a lesser punishment? It's not condoning the wrongdoing, but instead considers morally whether the punishment fits the crime because of the circumstances. Does that make sense?

Being Equitable is, hand-on-heart, one of the biggest things you've got to be as you go through this business. We're big believers in karma; what goes around comes around. When people do others a disservice, it will come back to bite them at some point in the future. You can guarantee it. So, be Equitable.

The True Hidden Secret Of Property Investment

Moving on, let's say the market value of the property is £100,000. We can get a 75%, buy-to-let mortgage on it. That's 75% of its market value, so keep that in mind as we go through these examples. The refurbishment works cost £7,000, and there's the cost of buying it, of stamp duty and legal fees etc. of £6,500. So, we've got around £13,500 of costs that are going into this deal, regardless of the price we pay for it.

If we can get a 75% loan-to-value buy-to-let mortgage based on the market value, that would give £75,000, as the ceiling price. Working back from that figure, if we've got £13,500 worth of costs, the maximum purchase price we could pay would be £61,500. Now, people say, "How the hell do you buy a £100,000 property for £61,500?" The point is, it usually requires some work doing to it and circumstances to align, such as the property going to auction, or it hasn't sold for whatever reason, or it's a distressed sale.

For example, let's say the chain fell through where someone is emigrating to Australia tomorrow and they need to sell, this might be one of the reasons why they'll sell at a discount (amongst many others). When the market value is £100,000, and you spent £61,500 to buy it, you spend £13,500 on doing it up and the costs of acquisition, and you can refinance the deal at £75,000, can you see why this is a very different scenario to the amateur who pays 13%+ above market value for the exact same property?

This is the secret magic pill of property investment: **where the deal refunds your total costs of £75,000 and gives you £25,000 in equity.**

This is where the light bulb goes on for most people, so it's worth repeating. You've spent £61,500 on the property. You spent £13,500 doing it up. Your total costs are £75,000. You get a 75% buy-to-let mortgage, which is £75,000, but the market value is £100,000, so, you've now got £25,000 of equity and all your money back.

You've effectively got a property (and an income) for free! Powerful stuff. And if you've got a property and an income for free, how many deals can you do following the same format?

How Can I Be Sure What It's Worth?

To dive a bit deeper into this concept, let's say we're looking at a particular street in a town that we know is going to be great for buy-to-let investment. To determine the value of the property, we need to look at comparable evidence which, to an estate or letting agent, is probably a bit like teaching your grandmother to suck eggs.

But just in case we might overlook something that could adversely impact your business, lets drill down on this further. From historic records of past sold prices, we know that one house sold in the street for £95,000 about six months ago, and another sold for £105,000 in reasonably good condition.

Then we've got another which made £97,000 and a fourth where the buyer paid £100,000.

When another property comes to the market in this area, what is its market value going to be? You can see we've got values ranging from £95,000, to £97,000, to £100,000, to £105,000. We can say with some confidence, assuming it's a similar type of property in a similar area, and similar condition, it's going to be worth c.£100,000.

So, can you see why buying at a discount locks in equity from day one? It's a super important principle to grasp, and if you're not familiar with these concepts, or if it hasn't quite clicked yet, please go over and over this part of the book, because once it clicks, you'll realise why it's the hidden secret to property investment. It's also why Robert Kiyosaki says, "you make your money when you buy".

You also get the same rent for the property, regardless of what price you pay for it.

Hopefully you can see that by reducing your initial outlay to buy the property, your return on investment only goes up. Whether you pay £100,000 for it, or £50,000, the rental income will still be the same. Yet one will add to your wealth, whilst the other will detract from it.

How Can You Use This?

You now know that all your client's property deals should be cash flowing, and you also understand why a discount is crucially important to property investors. Now, having this at the back of your mind, how can you use this to rapidly grow your business? How could you use this to help your clients? Or could you use this to help yourself to start your own property portfolio in the background? Hopefully, if we've done a good enough job of explaining the concepts in this book, the answers are obvious.

Here's where things can get really juicy, so bear in mind this next secret can create untold income for your business. When you're finding these types of deals for people, investors will pay a minimum sourcing fee of £1,500+ per deal and each deal doesn't necessarily have to be discounted by 25% or more. Some armchair investors will happily pay a handsome sourcing fee just to get a deal at a discount to open market value. (As regulations are constantly changing, please make sure you are fully compliant with The Property Ombudsman regulations around property sourcing as well as any other organisations who may seek to regulate this market now or in the future).

Also bear in mind, investors will pay someone (you), to project manage the refurbishment of each deal, especially if they live outside the area. They will quite happily pay a project management fee of £1,500+.

They'll also pay you to find a tenant. So, for each deal that crosses your desk, you've got the potential to make an extra £3,000-£4,000+ if you play your cards right. It's not that difficult to do, because the tenant find bit, you're already doing, right?

Think about this all from a property investor's point of view (your ideal target market). They buy a deal from you at a discount. They've made a profit at day one in terms of their equity in the deal, and they've got an income producing asset that cashflows for the rest of their lives. And they'll happily pay you at each stage of the process.

Do you think investors are going to stick with you for a long period of time if you're providing them with this type of invaluable service? Unless you do something drastically wrong, they're going to want to be handcuffed to your business with the most beautiful pair of golden handcuffs that money can buy!

What If I'm Too Busy?

Probably one of the worst things we hear people saying is they can't be bothered to learn these new strategies, or they're simply too busy with work at the moment, or they've got a lot going on with all the current regulatory changes to take any action. Yet underneath it all, they're scared to act on something new, or they think it doesn't apply to them, or it doesn't apply in their area.

Perhaps you're in central London, and you think, 'there's no way we can buy those types of properties at a discount. Well, the London market may well be declining soon as people move out of the city, but the point is, what if you've got investors who earn a lot of money in London and who want to become armchair investors? You may have a lot of wealthy clients you can work with, who might be interested in building a portfolio hands-off, in a different part of the country.

The question is, can you help them achieve that? Could you start to build connections (via the WiggyWam marketplace) agents in different parts of the country where you can bring a steady stream of investors to the area? Could you help to find properties for your clients and then help project manage each refurbishment project? Yes, you're helping to build up your client's wealth, but you're also building yours at the same time. Do you think an investor might pay you £1,500 to make £15,000+ in equity from day one? Is that not a fair exchange? When you get this right, they'll probably pay you quite a bit more.

A lot of agents then think, they can't project manage a refurbishment, but the simple point is, you don't have to or be on site every single day (unless you want to). You can act as a high-level project manager whilst the day-to-day builder does most of the project management and you're the go-between for your client. Start nurturing the contacts you've got in the industry and use them to help get your business flying.

How Many Of Your Competitors Will Bother?

If you're brutally honest, you'll realise hardly any of your competitors will bother doing this. Which gives you a massive head start. It's also why we've personally witnessed those businesses which do take action, grow far quicker and faster than their competition. Do you think landlords will stay with you long term if you help them build their business in a hands-off fashion, where they don't have to go out and do all the negotiating, because you've already secured the property for them?

True, they might have to leave a few thousand pounds in the deal, but you've saved them all the hassle and hard work of finding it and you're charging them a fee for doing so. You can then assist with the project management of the refurbishment and find them a tenant once it's done. All they've got to do is get the mortgage (which you may be able to assist with using a friendly local mortgage broker), and they're away…

You can also use this to build your own wealth via your own portfolio, which is something not to be overlooked. As you make more money in your lettings business, it should give you more money to grow your own portfolio. How much difference do you think it will make to put £3,000+ in your back pocket every time you have a new property to rent out? Even if you only did one property deal a month, how much difference would that extra income make to you and your family over the course of a year? An extra £36,000 a year is not to be sniffed at!

Fatal Mistake Number Three - The failure to take action.

We feel this is a huge mistake which undermines a lot of agents in their business - the failure to take any action (especially on what's presented in the Estate Agents Secrets series). Agents will say, "I've heard all this sort of stuff before, and it doesn't apply to me. There's no deals in our area. There are no investors. The market's too crazy right now etc." They vomit all these excuses out as to why this isn't going to work for them and their business which creates a stalemate situation.

We can't twist anybody's arm to get out into the market and take action to implement this; it's down to those who want this to take action if they feel it's right for them. Those who don't act, tend to have small businesses and they also lack leverage.

We see a lot of agents not maximizing their contacts enough; most of you naturally have access to a ton of contacts professionally such as, builders, electricians, painters, decorators, etc., a perfect trades team to go in and quickly refurbish properties for your clients to rent out.

This might sound harsh, but we believe that by failing to act on what you've learned from this book, you're potentially putting your clients at risk of financial harm in the future, and they don't even know it. They don't realize it because interest rates have been low for a long period of time, so they're not stress-testing their deals. These are very valuable secrets you can bring to the table to really help them with their business. So, we feel you have an ethical and moral obligation to help them with this new-found knowledge.

We've talked about interest rates rising, which will devastate cashflows and potentially leave investors in harm's way. These are things you need to share with your clients. It's better for them to be forewarned, forearmed, and prepared, rather than going headlong into economic uncertainty and then finding out their portfolio doesn't work. There's also the most overlooked factor in business to consider – the referral network of each satisfied client who may also choose to do business with you once they hear a strong recommendation from a trusted friend.

You're also letting thousands of pounds a month (if not tens of thousands), slip through your fingers and you don't even realize it. So, we implore you to act on this right now (book your call using the link above – you have nothing to lose and everything to gain).

A Big Reason Why

Let's be frank, we view estate and letting agents as far more professional, and as such, have a higher standard and duty of care than some property investors who are sharks and charlatans, who will simply try to rip people off. From that point of view alone, we encourage you to use this to grow your business, because it will really help improve the overall standard of the property industry and you could save a lot of people from getting hurt.

As a quick share, the first investment property we were going to buy in 2003 (having read some property investment books), was a three-bedroom bungalow in Adelaide, Australia (on the other side of the world from the UK). When we look back, it was complete nonsense to even contemplate this, but we had a little knowledge and didn't know any different at the time! It cost us £4,500 to get out of that deal and to <u>not</u> buy the property.

We're so glad we pulled out, because could you imagine the hassles of having such a property abroad? You're completely reliant on a letting agent who's 12 hours ahead of you and who may not have the same ethical or moral compass as you. It could have been an absolute nightmare, but we didn't know any better. The point is, your clients may be making potentially catastrophic financial decisions without even realising it because they don't have access to the same information that you do, because you've read these books.

Next Steps

Here's what you need to do to take baby-steps towards implementing these secrets in your business immediately. First, practice the cashflow calculation at least 100 times.

The best way to do this is to pick random properties on your books, or on one of the property search engines. Practice on 100 different properties, so you have a very good understanding of the numbers. Then, when you sit in front of your clients and you run the numbers on their portfolio, you can truly show them you know exactly what you're talking about, and you won't be stumbling all over your words. Notice which properties work and which don't because that will be a key indicator to success.

A word of warning, you might notice in some parts of the country (maybe even your area), these cashflow calculations don't work, because the cost of acquiring the property is too high and the rent won't cover the mortgage. That's important to notice as it may determine the areas where you suggest your investor clients build their portfolio's.

Once you've done 100 cashflow calculations, start reaching out to clients to offer this as a service. Don't forget to factor in 6% base rate to their portfolio to see how it will function if interest rates continue to rise.

Then, start to build a list of where to find great deals which we'll show you more about in the next section.

And finally, don't forget, we're here to help you anyway we can:

If you want to know how you can really add value to your clients and your business, there's a ton of extra resources we can share with you on a call.

We just ask you to invest 30 minutes into a complimentary consultation, where we can help fast-track your success (with no hard sell whatsoever).

Here's the link to book your call:

http://www.wiggywam.co.uk/estateagentssecretscall

CHAPTER SEVEN

THE SECRETS TO FINDING
GREAT DEALS

Before we get into the renovation and refurbishment process, it's important to know where to find the best deals which you can pass onto your clients in exchange for a handsome fee. We encourage all agents reading this to charge a fair sourcing fee to ensure your time invested is repaid, but also you get the benefits of repeat business when your client feels well taken care of.

One step to take before you get into sourcing is to find out which of your clients are still actively looking for property deals. Now this won't be everyone in the current climate, but there will always be a hardcore group of investors who will still want to invest and acquire new deals. Also remember that not everyone will want the same type of property, nor have the same investment strategy, so it's worthwhile carefully interviewing potential clients to understand their needs to match suitable properties to them. There will also be those people who are scared their pensions will soon be worthless with the stock market crashing, so it may be easier to find buyers for deals than you first thought.

However, ensure you are working with competent legal, and professional financial advisors if you want to go down this route, so you're keeping yourself on the right side of the law. This includes the requirements of The Property Ombudsman in relation to property sourcing compliance.

As the economy begins to get tougher, seller's behaviour will begin to change. There will always be a certain part of the market who will want to try and save on agency fees by doing the work of trying to sell their home themselves. So, be on the lookout for what we call FSBO's (pronounced Fuzz-bo's), which means For Sale By Owner.

First of all, let's take a look at some of the places we've suggested property investors use to find great deals. For some, this will be a huge insight into how investors' minds work, so for maximum benefit, we're sharing it completely unedited from the secret investor handbook we created to assist investors on their journey. Then, we'll share with you the top tips to renovating and project-managing properties for your sourcing clients and claiming a sizeable fee for your efforts.

Secret Investor Handbook Extracts – Finding Great Property Deals

(To preserve the authenticity of the message, we've included it in its entirety).

The below are sources to investigate if you want to find the best deals in your chosen investment area. Keep in mind that you'll revisit these sources again and again over the coming months and years as you build your business, so please don't mistakenly think that once you've explored a potential source once, that's the hard work done.

What's that saying about the mother of all skills being repetition....?

- **Letting Agents:** Whilst most new investors try to deal exclusively through estate agents, the smart investors know that letting agents also deal in property and will know some of their clients may be looking to sell their properties. If you offer to leave the property with the agent to manage once you buy it, they'll more than likely arrange an introduction to the owner.

- **Owner's Selling Properties Themselves (FSBO's):** The 2008 recession created a market for people trying to sell their property themselves without paying agency fees. These properties are easy to identify as they usually have a hand painted 'For Sale' sign outside or even worse, a piece of paper stuck to the upstairs bedroom window with 'For Sale' written on it in pencil! These can be a great source of deals, however, make sure you're treating the sellers with respect as many of them won't be trained in the art of negotiation or house buying and selling. They will need some guidance from you as to what's involved and how quickly they can expect to move. Look after them and they will look after you.

- **Private Adverts In The Newspaper Classifieds:** Amateur landlords and sellers will try and save money on agent's fees by advertising properties themselves in the newspaper. Call these people and see if they are open to selling their properties. You never know where it can lead! You can also place your own advert in the newspaper telling people you want to buy local properties, which may generate calls from those who want to sell but don't want to use estate agents for whatever reason.

- **Leaflet Drops:** Use these to target areas you want to buy properties in but make sure you're distributing leaflets to the doors in the area at least every other month. Also, be sensible and selective over where you are leafleting. Whilst it may sound great leafleting 100,000 properties, the costs of doing this on a regular basis will be unsustainable and its unlikely you'll get better results than targeting an area of 10,000 homes, 10 times a year. Research has shown that a person must see your marketing message a total of 7 times before they consider acting on it.

- **Talking To People & Prospecting:** One of our mentors is a huge fan of talking to people <u>all the time</u>. He talks to everyone and makes sure they end up with his business card, letting them know that he buys houses. He will talk to anyone in an area whether he meets them in the local shop, a property networking event, or the local pub. We encourage you to do the same, as you never know where it will lead. The good thing about the Great British public is that everyone loves to talk about property, and you may well get a lead to one of their friends who is looking to sell their house quickly and who will accept a good offer on it.

- **Social Media:** Social media has given people the chance to gain lots of exposure for themselves and potentially their property if they are trying to do the marketing on their own. Be on the lookout for property-related posts in your local social media groups and ask your friends to tag you in any that they notice which might be of interest to you.

- **Adverts On Supermarket/Shop Notice Boards:** Some people's idea of marketing is to write a small card or note and place it on a supermarket notice board or in the window of their local shop to find a buyer or tenant. This can be hugely ineffective and fraught with potential problems from unscrupulous individuals, so we would encourage you, as an ethical investor, to make contact and assist them where possible.

As you patrol your investment area, you must visit and revisit these potential sources several times to be effective. The rewards for this repetition are enormous. Just one deal a year from any of these sources will pay for your time, effort, and energy.

We're quite sure you can come up with your own possible sources for deals too, so take a moment to jot down a few more areas where you might be able to find great deals where your competition aren't even looking:

The Renovation and Refurbishment Process

By now, you should have a clearer understanding of the secrets of how to find great deals. The part of the process we're going to cover now is the one single area where most new investors really sink themselves and cost themselves a fortune. By understanding the renovation and refurbishment process and what's involved from a project management perspective, you can help your clients avoid expensive headaches and put money in both your pockets.

Despite the fact that programmes such as Homes Under The Hammer and

DIY SOS have made renovating a property look easy, the reality is you're going to be faced with quite a few challenges that need to be met head-on for the project to succeed. Some of you may be tempted to think you can short-cut the process by making offers on properties that are already done up, but the problem with this is, you're not adding any value to it so your client may not be able to refinance it to recover their costs and/or their deposit. So ideally, the properties you're looking for will require some renovation to increase their value. You will also find it easier to buy distressed properties at discounted prices as you can justify a lower offer because of the level of work required, which puts most other buyers off.

A major problem people face when renovating an investment property is the desire to do it to their own tastes rather than what's required to suit the local market. The danger here is the emotional attachment which causes people to overspend by putting a Jacuzzi bath in the bathroom and installing a 'Christies Kitchen' with built in appliances and granite worktops in a two-bedroom terraced house in Hull!

Now this may sound extreme, but we've seen many examples where new investors have been swayed by their emotions to buy and install more expensive kitchens and bathrooms which all adds to their costs and detracts from their bottom line. Also, your personal tastes may well be opposite to what the market actually wants, so you'll find it harder to rent it or sell it if you've gone against the grain.

Remember, property renovations need to be 'fit for purpose' and you aren't going to be living there yourself. That does not mean doing a substandard job or offering poor quality accommodation. The standard you're aiming for is one where you would be happy to live in the home yourself.

If you listen to your intuition, you will not provide squalor, nor will you renovate to the standard of Buckingham Palace! It will be to a good standard; clean, tidy, and presentable; a blank canvas where your tenants or buyers can create a home rather than living with your chosen mark of individual feature wallpaper and chintz.

Another big mistake people make is the order of the renovation works as most new project managers lack experience. To keep you safe in the process, let's look at how to do it:

- **Strip out and 'demolition' – Timescale 1-3 days –** We don't suggest trying to take on too much work for your first couple of projects. Such projects can become money-pits which drain your client's cash reserves if you don't know what you're doing, or if you don't have reliable trades you can count on who will quote accurately for each job. However, some properties may require the removal or repositioning of an internal wall to improve the layout of the accommodation. If you're planning on doing this type of work, please ensure you've consulted with a structural engineer, who can advise if any walls are load bearing or not. The last thing you want to do is remove a wall and the rest of the house collapses (believe it or not, this has happened). Strip out includes removing the existing kitchen and bathroom (assuming these are to be replaced), any old carpets, wallcoverings and flooring you're not planning to retain. During strip out, certain items of work may arise which were not immediately obvious during the initial inspection, so it pays to budget 15% more on top of your quoted renovation costs as a contingency to keep you and your client safe. If something does crop up that you weren't expecting, talk to your builder and find a solution. It goes without saying you must use a qualified Gas Safe engineer if the gas boiler needs replacement, repair, or servicing, or you plan on stripping out any gas appliances from the property. You don't want to put anyone at risk by trying to cut corners. This stage is also where the risk of injury to people is the highest, so keep an eye on the site to ensure the trades are exercising the appropriate caution to avoid accident or injury.

- **Damp-Proofing Works – Timescale 1-4 weeks (including drying out time) –** Hand in hand with the strip out from the property is making a start on any damp-proofing works which may be needed. This will likely involve the removal of internal plaster to a height of around one metre to ground floor. Not only is this messy, but you'll also have to think about the treatment process which could involve injecting the walls with a damp-proofing solution, applying two render coats with a waterproofing layer in-between, and a plaster finish. Depending on the time of year, it could take several weeks to dry out, so if it's not started as one of the first jobs, it could affect the timescale to complete the property and get it let or sold. Get an established timber and damp-proofing specialist on the job who can provide a guarantee once it's complete.

- **Replacement External Doors and Windows – Timescale 1-3 days** – If the property has timber or old aluminium double glazed windows, it makes sense to replace them with uPVC double glazed windows which will be more energy efficient and make the property look good, so its easier to rent or sell. Shop around for the best deals as costs and quality can vary greatly. They need to be done early as the removal of old windows could damage internal plaster work which will need patching up. Also check to see if the openings need to have new lintels installed to support the brickwork, otherwise a lack of support could cause the brickwork to eventually sag onto the window, causing cracking, or even making it difficult to open or close the window. In line with Building Regulations, the contractor should be able to provide a FENSA certificate upon completion.

- **Rewiring and Repluming – Timescale 7-14 days** – If you're planning on doing any rewiring or replumbing at the property, it's wise to get your trades started on this work early once the strip out has been completed. It will almost certainly involve taking up some of the floorboards to run the wires and pipes throughout the property. Depending on the time of year, your chosen plumber may be very busy, so try and book all trades well in advance of starting the project. If it needs a full rewire, this can be a messy job, as the wiring ideally needs to be channelled into the wall. With plumbing, it pays to opt for plastic pipes rather than copper for two very good reasons. The first is that plastic is far easier to work with, so it will speed up the job. The second is that copper is valuable and if the property is empty at any point, thieves may break in and strip the copper out to sell it, leaving you with substantial water damage. Use a qualified Gas Safe plumber to install the boiler and provide an installation certificate. As an agent, you appreciate the annual gas safety check is a legal requirement and without it, your client could be open to prosecution. Any new electrical work should also come with an NICEIC compliant installation certificate certifying the works have been undertaken in line with modern Building Regulations. Please note, it's illegal for anyone to do any work to domestic wiring who is not Part 'P' registered.

- **Plastering – Timescale 7-14 days** – The extent of any plastering will naturally reflect the extent of work done and the state of the existing walls. Not all internal walls or ceilings may need doing, but sometimes it's worth spending a little extra time and money now on replastering the whole property, so it's in good order for the next 10-15 years. One secret tip if you're considering replastering the ceilings, is to overboard them with a new layer of plasterboard. It saves a ton of dust and mess by not removing the existing ceiling and is far quicker. Remember, you'll need to allow a few days for the plaster to dry out before you can start painting and this is essential, or you'll end up with stains in the paint finish, or worse, cracking the new plaster. Prioritise the order of the rooms you want to replaster with particular focus on the kitchen and bathroom areas first, especially if you're installing a new bathroom suite or kitchen. This should allow the plaster to dry out whilst other trades continue with their work. It also gives them smooth, flat walls to work up to. Another hidden secret from a very experienced plasterer, is to ensure all plasterboard joints are covered with board-bonding and scrim cloth. This binds the boards together, so you don't end up with 'hairline cracking' on the joint line, which not only looks unsightly, but completely defeats the object of plastering in the first place if you're going to have to rake out the joint, fill it with Polyfilla, sand it down, and then decorate! It is a huge frustration when plasterers ignore this hack, but by the time it shows up, they'll be long gone with your cash and you're the one left with the problem. You should never accept shrinkage cracking as par for the course and if a plasterer is not willing to put scrim cloth and board-bonding on the joints, get another plasterer!

- **Installation of the new Kitchen or Bathroom – Timescale 7-14 days** – Once the plastering is finished, the installation of the kitchen and bathroom can begin. One school of thought is to always opt for kitchens, which come ready assembled, so they're quicker and easier to fit on site. This is good logic, but the budget may drive the decision. The bathroom suite should really be a white three-piece suite comprising bath, toilet, and wash basin, which can be readily obtained from trade suppliers and aren't expensive. Go for pressed-steel baths rather than acrylic; the latter flex too much once weight is applied which causes more stress to the silicone sealant and may lead to water leaks. Another top secret tip is to always go for the best quality silicone for the bathroom (you will know it's the best quality silicone as you won't believe the price of it compared to the cheap stuff!), because water leaks can cause a ton of damage which can be easily avoided.

- **Timberwork – Timescale 3-10 days** – Hopefully, the project will not require complete replacement of the door frames, architrave, or skirting boards, so any new timber will need to match the existing where it may be missing or rotten and hanging new internal doors. New timberwork should be delayed until <u>after</u> any plasterwork has dried out, otherwise the kiln-dried timber may absorb excess moisture in the air (from the plaster drying out), and warp. Dehumidifiers aide the drying-out process, as does leaving the windows slightly open, but be careful not to dry things too quickly (with the use of intense heat for example) which may cause cracking.

- **Decoration – Timescale 7-14 days** – Decorating the property should be one of the last jobs once all the dust and mess has finished. New plaster should be given a 50/50 mix of water and trade emulsion paint applied as a base coat, which will be quickly absorbed by the new plaster but should not cause cracking. If you apply undiluted paint straight onto new plaster, it may crack or even fail to stick. Keep the colour scheme as simple as possible. Using trade paint is not expensive and will provide good cover for the money. It's likely the walls and ceilings will require 2-3 coats if you're painting new plasterwork; a 50/50 base layer, followed by 2 coats of undiluted emulsion. White gloss paint to timberwork is sensible as it is easier to clean, and it looks good. Before the painter applies the new paint however, make sure they're giving all surfaces to be painted a quick rub down with some sandpaper to provide a 'key' (rough surface), for the paint to stick to and there's no dust present when they're decorating.

- **Finishing Touches – Timescale 1-5 days** – The finishing touches will be things like the installation of ironmongery to doors, lamp shades to lights, and laying new carpet or vinyl to the property in the appropriate areas. They make it look homely. Use reasonable quality, hard-wearing carpet throughout which will provide excellent wear. Consider using the same colour carpet throughout to keep costs down and go for a darker colour so it doesn't show marks as much as lighter coloured carpet might.

Using the above as a guide should help to ensure the different trades are not falling over one another on site. On the average three-bedroom, two-storey terrace, (the staple diet of most property investors), the renovation process should take no longer than 4-6 weeks. Have upfront discussions with your builder about payment for their services and make it clear you won't be giving them any money up front. If they say they need money for materials to start the job, get them to order the materials whilst you pay for them and get them delivered to site so they're in your control and ownership. There are many horror stories of people who have trusted a rogue builder to their detriment and have been ripped off to the tune of thousands of pounds.

When working with builders and tradies, align your attitude to them with your expectations. What we mean here is best shown via some examples. Take Fred, an amateur investor who has the belief he cannot trust anyone and believes all builders are out to rip him off. Unsurprisingly, this becomes his experience. He talks about how he has sacked tradesman after tradesman which cost him an additional £20,000 over the last three projects plus delays as he was unable to find people to complete work for him. His attitude leads to him working with people who match his thinking – i.e. they all rip him off and no-one can be trusted! Interesting…

Let's contrast this with Thomas, a professional investor who has worked hard to build a team of reliable tradies to deal with a regular number of projects whilst he spends his time identifying more deals. He was quick to establish a template in the beginning so everyone knew what was expected, leaving little room for surprises or changes in the spec along the way. This led to the builder and tradies working seamlessly together on site, so each project was completed on time and within budget. The approach of trusting his team until they proved otherwise has served him well and allowed him to save lots of time and money over the last two years of building his Buy-to-Let portfolio.

If you want to know how you can really add value to your clients and your business, there's a ton of extra resources we can share with you on a call.

We just ask you to invest 30 minutes into a complimentary consultation, where we can help fast-track your success (with no hard sell whatsoever).

Here's the link to book your call:

http://www.wiggywam.co.uk/estateagentssecretscall

CHAPTER EIGHT

THE SECRETS TO EXPLOSIVE GROWTH IN YOUR BUSINESS

Let's talk about a secret concept which has the potential to completely revolutionise and turbocharge your business. Before we do however, this is not a concept that we've just pulled out of thin air and invented, we simply 'stood on the shoulders of giants' to learn this technique from such people has Dana Derricks and Chet Holmes.

The Dream 100 is probably the most powerful secret methodology to employ in your business. It's amazing how well hidden this is as an industry secret, but once you learn it, you'll understand why. It literally has the power to bring you more work than you can possibly handle.

Does that sound like fun?

So, what is the Dream 100 and how do you go about making it work in your business?

Let's look again at the typical client acquisition process of most agents. Most estate agents will literally wait on calls from members of the public who invite them to their property and give them a valuation. And here's the important bit; they're literally waiting on dribs and drabs of one client per phone call, who they go out to provide a service to, and get paid for delivering that one-on-one level of service.

Occasionally an estate agent will drop lucky and will get into bed with a property developer who may do more than a couple of deals a month or who may be able to bring them a substantial block of work as they've just bought a building site, so they'll be selling 7-10 units with them next year. This offers

111

a great opportunity for the estate agent because they're winning a bigger number of instructions from one client. However, the problem is, most developers are usually broke, so as a consequence, may try and screw the agent down to $3/4$ of a percent or less.

So, the question is, how do you consistently win more business than you can possibly handle at very comfortable fees?

The key is to target clients who can bring you a large volume of property business.

For example, in our local area, an agency exploded their business because they made a point of servicing a local housing association who had over 10,000 properties under management. The housing authority decided to offload a lot of their old stock at auction so they could buy new houses from local developers. They were effectively swapping their old stock for new.

Being a housing association, they could buy the new housing at a substantial discount and as the housing association had inherited their stock from the local authority, it didn't cost them much to begin with. What impacted their stock the most was the costs of maintenance to run the properties, which disappeared once they got rid of the older, tired, worn out, and draughty properties and exchanged them for brand-new, double-glazed and centrally heated units which need minimum maintenance.

The impact of winning this one client was astronomical. The Housing Association were offloading anywhere between 10 and 20 units per month via their local auction. Even if there was some fee negotiation to account for volume, the properties were popular with local people who thought they were going to snap up a bargain.

Because of the sheer volume, they put in place economies of scale, such as regular viewing slots for 30 minutes leading up to the auction and all the punters knew the drill – turn up at the allotted time or lose out. They'd advertise the properties at about a third of their true market value as the guide price, whip up a frenzy of interest, pack the auction room to the rafters, and drop the hammer on almost every lot every single month. It became a seamless operation that led to further opportunities to let and manage the properties as they were sold to investors, or even sell owners homes when something interesting came up in the auction.

In short, just securing this <u>one</u> relationship helped the estate agent make a ton of money and explode their business. So the question is: Was it worth it?

Hopefully there's a few fireworks going off in your brain right now suggesting ideas where you are, or could be, well placed to deal with certain players in your local market. The question then remains, how do you get hold of such people? This is something we'll explore in greater detail as we go through this chapter.

The first exercise is to grab a piece of paper, or spreadsheet on your computer, and start making a list of all of the local organisations who could provide you with a substantial book of work if you could get a working relationship going. We mentioned a Housing Association previously, however you might look at charities who deal with a lot of properties, or the Local Authority who has housing stock that needs disposing of. There may even be military bases or large businesses who help provide housing for their staff.

A quick story for you - when we first got into estate agency, our firm took on an ex-RAF base to sell off their properties. Although the base didn't have the best of reputations, those houses were quite possibly the biggest bargains ever missed out on because when they come up for sale, few people wanted to live there. They were sold off for anywhere between £20-40,000, yet they were very substantial three-bed semi-detached homes with good size gardens and parking.

Over the course of 10 years, the price of these properties trebled as more private owners took them on, and started to soften the look of the area by making them comfortable homes to live in. They also reaped the rewards as the houses were then selling for £120,000+…

Bearing in mind what we talked about earlier, these properties would have made great investments as buy-to-lets as they were well-built and had plenty of space so they would have attracted a premium. Imagine securing one of these homes for yourself or your clients and watching your investment balloon in value over a short period! How happy would you all be?

Going beyond this, start to think about other unique areas where you can help businesses such as utility companies, or maybe such organisations as the HS2 rail network, or network rail who may have properties which they may need to sell and which would make a big difference to your business if you were the only agent to win the instruction.

Ideally, you want to get to at least 100 names on your list – hence the name, the Dream 100.

Getting Past The Gatekeepers

Once you've made your list, the second stage is working out how to contact them to start building the relationship. This has to be done tactically if you're going to get past the gatekeepers and speak with the decision makers who can put business your way. You'll have to do some groundwork to kick the door open and start building the relationship, especially if they may not take too kindly to cold calls or unsolicited letters.

In his book The Ultimate Sales Machine, Chet Holmes covers an enormous amount of strategies which he employed to kick the door firmly open and make this secret strategy work for him and his company. One of the key things Chet used was a multi-faceted approach. One involved a phone call where he called to offer a free gift to the head of department he wanted to speak to. This usually helped to get past the gatekeeper or at least get the name of the person concerned. Once he had their name and address, he employed a second tier to his strategy called lumpy mail!

Now consider the human psychology of most big hitters in an organisation when they're faced with receiving lots of mail from people essentially begging for your business. You probably receive the same from would-be suppliers to your business too, right?

As we all have an insane amount of pressure in our day-to-day diaries, most people naturally just throw these letters in the trash, or shred them, and will not take the time to reach out and connect with the suppliers even though they might need what's being offered.

Getting over this indifference can be quite frustrating when you're trying to get this tactic working initially because if you don't get it right, you'll be faced with making a lot of phone calls or sending a lot of letters to your targets which simply don't get through, resulting in zero response. So, it's very easy to give up.

But let's consider the emotional reaction to receiving lumpy mail in the post. The gatekeeper guards the big boss and sometimes proves almost impossible to get round. Most of them also answer their mail on their behalf. They'll open, sort (file under 'B' for bin!) and respond to the mail as part of their usual workday. But when the big boss receives a personally addressed lumpy mail envelope or parcel, most secretaries will be very wary about opening it and will pass it straight to them, especially if its marked private and confidential…

In essence, what you're doing is sending small gifts in the post to your target, and in doing so,, putting yourself in a very strong position, because not only are you instantly by-passing the gatekeeper, you're breaking up the hum-drum of the working day by using the element of surprise. They receive a small gift and don't instantly know who it's from. Do you think they will at least take the time to open the package, and when they're confused about why someone would be sending them a gift, at least give some attention to the package insert which explains why you're sending it to them?

It's called a pattern-interrupt, and it breaks them out of their workday by putting everything else to one side whilst they satisfy the curiosity of this unexpected package, and scratch that mental itch to know what its all about.

Now these gifts don't have to be expensive, but the point is they bypass the gatekeeper and make a lasting impression on the client. Think about it, who else in their right mind would send a prospective client a small gift in the post if it wasn't designed to grab their attention? Can you see your competition doing this…?

This works even better when combined with a cheeky message which matches the gift. For example, let's say you sent a small battery-operated torch, the type that somebody could easily attach to their keychain and use in the winter to help find their way to their car. You could use a clever message such as, "searching in the dark to find the right agent to sell your property? Please call Joe Bloggs on 01234 567891 to see the light…"

Now, assuming the first message doesn't generate the response you want, don't give up. Your second item of lumpy mail a few weeks or months later might be something such as a small pull-out tape measure with the clever slogan; "is your current agent struggling to measure up to the competition? Call us today to arrange a free executive briefing on how to solve your most pressing property headaches."

It's so important to not get disheartened if the first couple of lumpy mail items don't get the response you want. It's perfectly natural, so take the time to map out a 12-month contact calendar where you'll continue to send some small gifts to your prospective clients in a bid to pique their curiosity and get them on board to work with you.

As an example, let's say you aim to send one lumpy mail package per month, together with one letter two weeks later and a phone call every week. You can space these contacts out throughout the month, so you can start to make inroads into your Dream 100 list. With all the postage and packaging, plus the cost of the items concerned, you're not looking at spending an absolute fortune, but what you are doing is opening the door to a huge amount of potential business if you can land just one of the clients on your list.

It is not an exaggeration to say the Dream 100 secret strategy has the potential to literally blow the doors off your entire business and give you more work than you can possibly handle. So, use this strategy carefully and build your business in such a way that there's scarcity value in working with you. Scarcity equals demand, and demand means a healthy fee. After all, you've already proven how unique your approach is by using lumpy mail and persistence to open the door for you. Keep going for as long as it takes to win the business of your Dream 100 clients.

And one final note, once you win them over, it's tempting to not keep sending them packages because they're now your client. Don't fall into this temptation. If they're already doing business with you, keep them on the lumpy mail list – it's a reminder of what got your foot in the door in the first place and your clients will feel appreciated that you're still thinking of them.

The messaging may change slightly as you're not looking to win their business now, but the recognition of their value to you will help foster the goodwill between you both and will hopefully lead to more recommendations and referrals. And depending upon the amount of business they're bringing you, the value of those gifts may increase to such things as televisions, stereo systems, smartphones or iPads, or vouchers for meals in swanky places. Imagine paying for someone's dinner in a smart place and the whole topic of conversation is just you and your business. That's marketing you cannot buy!

CHAPTER NINE

SECRETS TO GAME-CHANGING GROWTH

Organic growth of your business is fine, but the unspoken secret to really move the needle in your business is doing growth via acquisitions. This is where you simply buy up your competitors' businesses, or other companies in different locations, expanding your reach.

If you're looking to grow through acquiring other companies, there are many things to consider so you avoid buying a lemon! It's one of the hardest things to do, assuming you want to buy it at a fair price and not overpay for it. There's plenty of people who overpay for a company in an attempt to grow rapidly, but many times this comes undone later on.

Like property investing, if you intend to acquire, do not be disheartened if you're making lots of offers on many businesses only to see them refused, rejected, or turned down. It is not an exaggeration to say you may need to look at 100 companies to buy one. That said, you'll be glad you took the time to get the right one as many are unprofitable or have major (cashflow), problems which may not be apparent on the accounts, but which become abundantly clear when you start to do a little digging. The last thing you want to do is acquire a business which becomes a noose around your neck giving your sleepless nights, or worse, leading you towards financial ruin!

To give you an example, we were recently introduced to a law firm which we were told had quite high debt i.e. £700,000 and the company was distressed because of personal problems the owner was experiencing. The numbers didn't frighten us, so we went and met the owner who was the most personable chap you could ever hope to meet. Despite the problems, he seemed particularly obliging to help and support us in buying the business, going so far as to say that he was very open, honest, reliable, and honourable.

During the first meeting, we managed to strike the broad outline of a deal and it was at this point he suggested we move quickly towards working together to take over the business as he was feeling too much pressure personally and wanted to leave asap (he was heading for a nervous breakdown). Being kind and caring, we decided to go ahead and work alongside the seller over the next couple of weeks to complete the due diligence process as the contracts were being prepared. But, as with all things that involve lawyers, the contracts took an enormous amount of time to get done, when it should have been a simple and straightforward agreement.

Whilst working at the firm, we began drilling down into the numbers to grasp the full financial picture as monthly management accounts were not being prepared. As we did so, it became abundantly clear that its debt was way more than £700,000… The more we dug into it, we saw that the firm was behind on almost all of its financial obligations and had accrued an enormous debt in excess of £1.4 million!

Even worse, a big chunk of that debt was owed to a loan shark!

Can you imagine the problems it would have caused to buy this business only to find out its debt position was double what we'd been told initially, was well beyond being saved, and also had creditors who would've taken matters into their own hands to recover their cash even if the business had gone through administration? It just highlights how important due diligence is and you can never be too careful when assessing a potential purchase.

A lot of people hear stories like this, and it puts them off ever taking steps towards buying a business. Please don't let this example put you off; there are thousands of businesses sold every year which are successful deals, but they have been well managed and thoroughly investigated before the paperwork was signed.

The advantages of buying another company are huge; you can double, or even triple your turnover (and hopefully profit), very quickly; you get existing trained staff who can help you process a surplus of work; and you may even acquire a unique piece of technology which adds a different dimension to your business (such as Facebook acquiring WhatsApp). However, if you get it wrong, it can cause serious problems to your personal finances and mental wellbeing.

We have a tongue-in-cheek joke within our professional circles which is; Q: "How can you tell when a seller is lying? A: Their lips are moving!"

This may not apply to all sellers, but the majority will always over represent the good, and underestimate the bad, so you need to conduct a very thorough due diligence process to sort the facts from the fiction.

Building Safety Into The Deal

One of the ways to build safety into your deal negotiations, is to avoid the 'the cash in a suitcase scenario'. Some, if not all sellers have the naïve expectation that a buyer will simply come along and place a large suitcase full of cash on the negotiating table before signing the contract so they can disappear off into the night having sold their business.

With any sale and purchase of a business, there needs to be a handover period of at least a few months (where the seller shows you the ropes and you learn how it's all being run), depending on the type of business you're buying.

If you're familiar with the business, this training period may be shorter, however it's sometimes wise to make this training & handover period between 6-12 months at least. It helps to ensure the seller is on the hook in some way if they're trying to sell you a lemon.

This is especially true where the seller has agreed to an element of deferred payment in the negotiations (which we'll come onto later), as they will be much more aware of how they conduct themselves during negotiations. It focusses their mind on the fact that if they tell lies to secure a very favourable deal, they may not receive some, or all, of the deferred element if the business performs badly after it's been sold.

Staffing Issues

One thing to be aware of; staff get incredibly nervous when they find out the company they work for is up for sale. They fear they won't like the new owners, or they will lose their job once it's been taken over. As a result, productivity (and turnover) is likely to dip between 10-20% within the first three months of new ownership. Some staff will even go so far as handing in their notice as soon as they find out, because they're scared of what might happen.

When staff start to leave, gossip begins to spread like wildfire throughout the office which may result in other staff then handing in their notice. Obviously, this is something you want to avoid by keeping the deal highly confidential, and not announcing it to the staff until after it has happened. Sellers also get very protective of their staff and want to be confident in your ability to take over and manage the business in a way that protects them. So don't be surprised when sellers raise this as one of the requirements for a deal.

Move Quickly

Staffing issues aside, when being introduced to a prospective acquisition, you should sit down with the seller asap to understand their motivations for selling and whether they're serious, or if this is an ego-driven exercise to find out how much their business might be worth. You'd be amazed at how many times sellers will put a business up for sale, explore options with potential buyers for six months and then change their mind! You don't want to waste a lot of time and one of the biggest ways to waste time is working with (most) business brokers.

Like anything in life, there are very good business brokers and very poor ones. The poor ones will usually make you jump through a million hoops and hurdles whilst trying to get an offer from you before you've even seen the business or spoken to the seller. This can be a very lengthy and time-consuming process which is not without cost and can put you in a position where you work very hard to end up with zero to show for it.

The great brokers will work very proactively to bring you deals consistently and will do their very best to help you get a deal done asap. Most brokers don't usually get paid until the deal completes, so it's very confusing why many seem to actively stand in the way of getting a deal done. We can only assume this is because they've never bought or sold a business themselves so don't understand the motivations of both parties or the complexities of deal making. Sure, they intellectually understand it, but the difference between that and a deep knowing because you've gone through it yourself several times, is huge.

What Is It You Actually Want?

Before you go shopping for businesses, it's wise to work out what you want to buy. Unless the firm you're thinking about buying is in a similar location to your current firm, it's not worth buying smaller companies as they tend to be one-man-band outfits and once you've bought it and the owner leaves, you're left doing two people's jobs (unless it's profitable enough to bring in people to do the work on your behalf).

To make acquisitions worthwhile, usually the more expensive the firm, the bigger it is, so you'll have a more substantial workforce in place, potentially with an existing management structure there too. This means there's less work for you to do, as the existing processes are already in place being run by others. You can tweak the processes a little, or introduce new ones, but you don't have to do everything yourself from scratch.

If you're buying a profitable company, it's likely you'll be taking on some form of debt, either from a mainstream institution like a Bank, and/or a sellers 'note'. The sellers note covers any deferred element of the deal and it's wise to get them to help you finance the purchase of their business for several reasons.

(As you know, this is not financial advice and must not be construed as such – we're simply sharing what we would do in similar circumstances).

First, most banks will not lend much against most businesses unless there's tangible security (such as a building) they can use to help finance the deal.

Second, where the seller "lends" you the money on paper to buy their business, its likely you can negotiate a minimal interest rate or even waive interest altogether.

For example, you might defer £200,000 of the purchase price of the business and pay it to the seller in equal instalments of £50,000 a year over 4 years. If you were to try and get this funding from another source, it will likely come with an expensive interest rate attached and require a personal guarantee. The seller may agree to a deal on paper where you can pay them the cash over the four years without interest.

What's even more exciting is you can use a seller's note to fund 100% of the purchase price of the business, so you don't need a fortune to get started!

Third, you can structure the deal in such a way that its contingent on the business performing in a certain way. This works well when you're tying the seller into the business for a period of time for handover or working there after you've bought it. If the seller has made certain promises about the performance of it which you feel aren't achievable in the future, you can tie the deferred element to the performance of the business.

So, let's say you have a feeling the seller might leave and then set up in competition with you taking some key clients and staff with them when they go. As its difficult to enforce non-compete agreements (as they're essentially against the human right to earn a living), you can simply structure the deal contingent against the business performing as it has done for the last few years, and any loss of clients or staff to the competing business will reduce the amount of the deferred payments made to the seller, or the seller will have to pay the business an agreed fee for each client or employee they take with them. This focusses the sellers mind and protects you from rushing into something that you might later regret.

As an example, this literally happened at an agency we worked for several years ago. Remember the story where we had our wages cut and so went to their most feared competitor? Well at the time, we didn't know they'd been approached by a London based company who wanted to expand their empire through acquisitions. Yet despite the brainpower and financial standing of this company, the deal they struck was laughable!

Without giving too much away, the competitor we went to work for had five branches at the time, and the name of the company was the name of the business owner. The London agency only wanted to buy three of their offices whilst the other two were sold as a management buy-out (MBO). Yet bizarrely, the two MBO offices retained the name of the original owner, who was now employed on a huge salary working for the rebranded London-based firm. The MBO offices also covered some of the same areas as the newly acquired London firm offices.

What happened over the course of a few years was the original owner, whose well-known name was still appearing on many boards in the local area, funnelled a ton of Joint-Agency work into the MBO offices, and once his contract was up, left and opened up a new office in his own name next door to the office he'd sold! Suffice to say, a few years later the London agency were acquired by another competitor who trimmed the operation and essentially put the original business owner back into his old offices with his name above the door again having taken them for a ton of money when he'd sold the firm and bagged a huge salary to boot!

If only they had read this book, they could have saved themselves a lot of time, money, and heartache…

If you're taking on debt to acquire, run the numbers against at the cashflow to ensure there's enough to support the new debt payment (and stress-test the interest rates like we talked about earlier). The debt payments may be on a monthly or annual basis depending upon how you've agreed to structure them. The more pressure there is on expenses, the quicker the cashflow dries up. And if you can't keep to the payments you've agreed with the seller, you could be in trouble.

Getting Culture Right

More method in the madness of these Volumes should become abundantly clear to you now as we unfold this section. Remember when we talked about company culture in Volume I? Well now you're about to see why setting the standard is twice as important.

One of the hardest things to get right within any business is the culture as it underpins a huge amount of the success of any business. Now imagine you've been working hard in your firm to establish your mission, vision, and values. You've got everything in place, your staff are all singing from the same hymn sheet, and the company is ticking along like a well-oiled machine. You've finally reached the utopia of business heaven, but your ambition says that's not enough.

So, what do you do? You go out and expand your empire by deciding to buy another branch, or complete company to expand your reach. And all the hard lessons of getting your business into its current shape are long forgotten.

When you buy your new enterprize, you now have a whole bunch of other people who have been used to working towards a different mission, a different vision, and an entirely different set of values. Can you see where the problem is?

Bringing these two companies together will create a culture-clash and the impact of this can send ripples of discontent through both organisations. The point it though, you've set the standard, so it's down to you and your team to educate the new recruits into the way things are done. And that can take time, and result in some staff leaving who aren't in alignment with those values.

To combat this, you need to be mindful to invest heavily in management and training to get the culture right. The good news is, you've already got a template to work to in your existing business, so you're not starting from scratch. You should also have the existing SOP's, KPI's or CD's and working practices to refer to, and running the new staff through this training and education journey will bring them quickly up to speed.

And if you've already laid out a training journey within your WiggyWam private training suite in our learning centre, the staff will be able to get started on how you do things quicker than ever.

Valuing The Deal

Unlike valuing properties for sale, valuing a business can be very difficult. That said, in simple terms, a business is worth what someone is prepared to pay for it, even though this simple fact of market forces and supply and demand is lost on most sellers!

Another in-joke within professional business buying circles is: Q: "How much is a business worth? A: Take the number of directors, multiply it by £1,000,000 and there's your answer!"

Unlike a house where there's usually at least a couple of comparables to use as a yardstick to gauge value, businesses tend to be unique based on how they're run, how they win business, how profitable they are and how much debt or liabilities they're carrying. Other factors will include the balance sheet position and whether the company has a bunch of tangible assets or whether the entire business value is wrapped up in the category of "goodwill" (which is largely meaningless unless you're a mega-brand like Coca-Cola).

As a guide, a business in the real estate space may be worth anywhere between a 1-3 times multiple of profits, however more tech specialist firms which have largely automated processes could be worth a 10+ times profit multiple. Let's assume however that you'll be going for a more traditional business which would fall into the 1-3 times profit multiple range.

When assessing its true value, first look at its debt position and how much the company owes to a Bank or other creditors. With the recent spate of Bounce-Back Loans provided, almost all businesses have increased their debt position following the pandemic. We would then look at how the business is structured and whether it will suffer when the seller eventually leaves. For instance, are they the sole 'Business Development Manager' for the company and the one who everyone goes to with problems?

As a tip, at around £1,000,000 turnover, a business usually has robust management structures in place and is less dependent upon the seller of the business. This means it's easier for you to take over and for the seller to leave without having a major impact. There's usually enough staff to take up any slack and handle any issues without them all landing on your desk.

When you're looking at the numbers, check to see what amounts the seller has been taking out of the business. Sometimes when sellers employ brokers, they prepare numbers which include 'add-backs' to make the company look healthier financially. But that could mean there's little allowance for you to take a salary or to employ someone to replace the seller making the business less profitable. There's only so much you can do, so don't stretch too much trying to buy a business that isn't all that profitable.

Finally, any deal you do reach should stack the odds in your favour. If the business is doing £200,000 a year profit and you feel it's worth around £500,000 (a 2.5 times multiple), see if it can be done by putting as little cash down as possible. You might decide to make multiple offers which may allow you to pay more for the business over time but require less cash up front. Here's some example offers to explain what we mean:

Offer One: All Cash

A cash offer (subject to contract), of £300,000 payable upon completion of the purchase.

Offer Two: Part Cash, Part Seller Finance

An offer of £400,000, payable upon the following terms:

a) 10% cash paid upon exchange of contracts (£40,000)
b) 20% paid within 60 days of completion (£80,000)
c) Balance to be paid in equal instalments over the next 5 years, i.e. £56,000 per year on the anniversary of the completion date (£280,000).

Offer Three: Cash, Seller Finance with Balloon Payment

An offer of £500,000, payable upon the following terms:

a) 10% cash paid upon exchange of contracts (£50,000)
b) 15% paid within 60 days of completion (£75,000)
c) Annual payments of £50,000 a year for the next 5 years (£250,000)
d) Final balloon payment of £125,000 at the end of year 5.

Can you see how these different options may appeal to different motivations of the seller? It's important not to overcomplicate things, however each scenario may flush out different motivations. If they want all cash and a quick exit, they'd choose the first option assuming there's no other buyer willing to pay more, but if they want the most for the business and would welcome nice chunks of cash each year, the third option may be best.

By deferring the payments for as long as possible, you're giving yourself a greater chance of building up the business, making more money, and not starving the business of much-needed cashflow in the early stages. But bear in mind, the longer it goes on for, the more the seller may be exposed to risk, so this will have some bearing on the option they will choose to run with. And if there's a broker or other third party involved, such as an accountant who gets their cut largely on the cash part of any deal, they'll create all sorts of obstacles to the deal.

Hopefully you can see that accurately valuing a business is a bit of a 'moving feast' and over time, you'll get more of a feel for what a business is worth which will help you in your negotiations. It can be a fun and creative process but also frustrating when deals don't happen.

Funding The Deal

When it comes to buying a business, working out how to fund it is what puts a ton of people off trying to take this valuable step forward. For the same reason as buying anything, some people get put off by the idea because they reason they don't have all the cash sitting in the bank ready to go.

As we explore this section, it's important you understand that we're not financial advisors, nor are we giving you, nor are we qualified to give you, financial advice in any way whatsoever. We always encourage you to review your potential options with a suitably qualified professional in accordance with FCA guidelines. The information we're sharing here comes from our own learnings and personal experience and what works for us, may not actually work for you, so protect yourself by doing as much due diligence as possible.

We're going to explore some secret ways you can use to acquire a business from the obvious to hidden. Like all things, the amount of planning you put in place will ultimately affect the results you achieve so it's worthwhile going about raising funds for a business acquisition early in the process before you have a target acquisition in sight. Raising money before you need it will help you find the right funding partner who's not going to fleece you on all the fees or the equity arrangement because you need the money quickly.

Let's just touch on the difference between debt and equity right now as this is a strategic difference you'll have to consider when deciding how to pull a deal together. You'll also learn more about deal structure when we talk about the different financing options later on.

When we talk about debt, we're talking about a lender putting up the cash to fund part, or all of a transaction. This might be on a secured (i.e., with some tangible security such as a property which the lender can register a legal charge over so should you not pay the debt back, they'll seize the property to sell and recover what's owed), or unsecured basis (i.e. no tangible security provided). Depending upon who the lender is, whether it's a high street bank, or a private individual such as a friend, or the seller of the business themselves, there may or may not be interest payable, and they may not require a personal guarantee, so it's up to you to investigate as many avenues as possible to find the right lender for your transaction.

As a word of warning, most traditional lenders will almost always insist on you providing a personal guarantee. This is essentially you signing a piece of paper where you personally underwrite the amount you're borrowing, and if for whatever reason the deal doesn't work out the way you thought it would, or the company goes bust, you'll personally be liable for paying it back using whatever means necessary, (or potentially face personal bankruptcy). This is where most people get scared and start to envisage their home being repossessed and all their stuff thrown out onto the street! Take a deep breath if this is you, because if you plan carefully, there are measures you can take to stop this from happening.

Again, this is not financial advice, however the reason a lot of people get themselves into trouble is because they don't understand things like private Trusts and asset protection vehicles. They usually hold everything in their personal name which leaves them wide open to having everything taken off them if they are unfortunate enough to become involved in legal action against them for whatever reason.

Wealthy people understand how to protect their assets using asset protection structures designed specifically to keep assets out of their personal name and away from those who may wish to make claims against them. So, if you're in the fortunate position to have made a bit of money already, it's worthwhile investigating setting up a Trust or other asset protection vehicle, either in the UK or offshore, before you take the step of incurring more debt or taking on other liabilities. Such a structure may also help you in lowering any potential tax liability. Be mindful of such structures as you grow your business empire as they could help you to minimise any potential personal exposure.

Coming back to the debt versus equity discussion, equity is where an investor provides the cash you need to buy the business, but rather than putting a loan agreement in place with an interest rate, they may simply take a shareholding or equity stake in the business. This means they own a pre-defined amount of the company and usually comes with requirements for the investor to receive monthly financial updates and to attend monthly board meetings.

When you're 'giving up' equity in your proposed deal, remember that someone else may then be calling the shots. This may or may not pose a problem in the actual running of the company depending upon what additional resources might be brought to the table other than cash.

If you watch Dragon's Den, you'll see company owners offering equity stakes in their company in exchange for the cash investment, but the Dragons are also bringing their experience and connections to the table; both of which are potentially worth a lot more.

However, whilst it's sometimes great to take the cash to get the business off the ground, assuming it grows to the level you expect, your investor may want to sell it earlier than you wanted to, to recoup their investment. Or worse, if the business goes through a series of 'seed rounds' of funding, and more cash is taken into the company at each funding stage, the owner's equity stake gets diluted, sometimes until the owner is booted out of the company they founded or is simply left with next to nothing to show for their efforts! Not an ideal situation to be in.

So, be wary about taking equity investors on board unless you're the one calling the shots. Having someone else breathing down your neck every month and pulling the company in a different direction can be a heavy price to pay.

Secret Funding Sources

Now let's look at the different funding sources which might be available to you. Some will rely on your credit rating (which you can check by getting a copy of your statutory credit report from Experian, Equifax or TransUnion (formerly CallCredit) – personally, we feel it's better to go direct to these three companies and get paper copies of your statutory credit report as they supply the data to every other 'credit score checking service'), whilst others will rely on your creativity, sharp thinking, and the motivation of the lender in selling their company. The higher their motivation to lend, the better the deal you can negotiate.

Here's some of the different funding sources which may be available depending upon your personal situation (obviously this is not to be construed as financial advice – always speak to a suitably qualified person):

- **Savings:** Cash in the bank which you or your partner/friends/family have access to and are willing to invest into the proposed deal. This should never be more than you're willing to lose if it all goes wrong.

- **Credit Cards:** One of the most flexible and cheapest forms of borrowing you can get your hands on. Depending on your credit standing and the offers available, you may be able to secure funds at 0% for 12+ months which is handy for funding part of the deal, such as a down payment, or investment into the company. Some credit card companies will allow you to draw down funds directly into your bank account and you can move balances from one card to another to take advantage of lower rates of interest or better deals with other providers (called stoozing). Credit card providers may see investing in businesses as high risk, but for some strange reason, they will happily advance you money for home improvements, to go on holiday, or to finance a wedding…

- **Business Loan:** As the name suggests, you may be able to get a business loan from a high street, niche, or online lender who will provide various facilities, either to acquire a company or to help run it (such as an overdraft), or even to buy new digital or other assets to help you grow. This may be secured or unsecured and will more than likely require a personal guarantee.

- **Mortgage:** This can either be in the form of a remortgage of your existing home, an investment property you own, or a mortgage on any of the tangible property which may come as part of the deal such as an office building. This is likely to be secured although you may find some niche lenders who will do a 'floating charge' over a bunch of assets. This is where you pledge several properties as security, but the lender doesn't formally register a charge at Land Registry. They reserve the right to seize one or more properties to recover the debt if you default and will register their charges prior to taking action.

- **Crowdfunding:** This is becoming more commonplace since the last recession where investors who were keen to see a greater return on their cash chose to invest in people's ideas or businesses via crowdfunding platforms. They offer a lot of flexibility, so it's worth exploring to find out what works best for you.

- **Seller Finance:** We touched on this earlier, and as a recap, this is where the seller essentially provides you with a "loan on paper" in the form of a sellers note. This is likely to be the most flexible form of financing you can obtain and its usual for sellers to fund at least part of a deal because it's rare for buyers to be able to fund 100% of the purchase price from traditional sources.

- **Friends/Fools/Family:** These are people who care deeply about you and want to see you succeed, and who are more likely to provide you with cash on very reasonable terms. A word of caution however, taking money from friends and family can be the one thing which undermines your relationship the most, particularly if you don't stick to the original terms of the deal, you default, or the business gets wound up and your friend or family member loses out forever. So, tread very carefully here.

- **Angel Investors:** Angels are usually established businesspeople who have made a ton of money and who are keen to reinvest it at grass roots level in start-ups or other business ventures where they can see potential for a healthy return. There may even be certain tax breaks available to them for doing so. Like the investors on Dragon's Den, they may come with a ton of experience and contacts, but you may find your share of the deal gets diluted over time, particularly if the Angel wants to take an equity stake in the company.

- **Family Offices:** Similar to Angel investors, but they usually have access to much greater wealth and will be able to fund much bigger deals. Accessing them is very hard as they get swamped with tons of deals, so are very picky about which ones they go for.

- **Joint Ventures (JV) & Strategic Partnerships (SP's):** The beauty of a JV or an SP is there are no fixed rules as to how such an agreement could work in practice and no need for cash to change hands. For example, as an agent you could do a JV with a removals company to supply them with leads or even package up part of your service to include removals. Technically this is more of a revenue sharing arrangement, but there could be other angles you explore with JV partners that would allow you to fund the deal without a big outlay of cash, by selling additional services ahead of time.

- **Approaching suppliers to the business:** This is a little out of the box, however its worth thinking about approaching suppliers to the business to see if they will either part fund the acquisition or provide you with greater credit terms to help with the cashflow of the business. For example, if they'll extend credit terms from 30 to 90 days or allow you to make reduced payments for an agreed period, this can help you stabilise the cashflow position and build up some cash in the bank to take the pressure off. This applies where the business is in serious financial trouble and creditors are faced with either agreeing to a revised payment schedule, or not recovering anything if the business goes to the wall. Organisations such as HMRC can be particularly open to negotiating despite popular beliefs.

The above list is not exhaustive but hopefully it helped stimulate a few ideas in your own mind as to where you can find some funds to help you do deals or grow your business. A great exercise is to spend twenty minutes with a blank piece of paper, writing down all the different avenues you could use to potentially finance a deal.

The Deal Pie

This is a top-secret concept we were introduced to by a business mentor who talked about 'The Deal Pie'. It's pretty simple but incredibly effective at helping you overcome the internal dialogue of thinking you can't do a deal.

Imagine a pie chart which represents 100% of the purchase price of the target. As you start to formulate the deal, look at all the different funding avenues that might be available as forming each individual slice of the pie.

For example, say your target acquisition price was £1,000,000, which your mind might struggle to see how feasible it is to do. Your first slice of the pie might be using your own savings of £50,000, or 5% of the purchase price.

The next slice may be £150,000 business loan which you can raise against the business, (another 15%). The third slice might be friends and family putting another 5% into the pot, so you're now up to 25% of the total purchase price. You might then decide to approach the seller for the 75% balance and see what you can negotiate. They get 25% or £250,000 cash up front, and then the balance over a period of time.

The Earn Out

A key part of any deal is the earn out which we touched on earlier. Here, you're saying to the seller they'll get paid the balance of their sellers note through future profits. If the business is making £200,000 a year profit, you could agree to do a straight 50/50 profit share for the next 5 years to pay the balance, or you could agree a fixed payment over the same period, or even a mixture of the two.

The advantages of the earn out are substantial and are our personal favourite as it puts the seller on the hook for a large proportion of the sale price. If the business isn't what they made it out to be, then there won't be any profits or cash in the business to make these payments. The converse is also true, and a seller will be wary about agreeing to an earn out as they may not recover the balance if you run the firm into the ground, or you spend all the cash on fast cars and expensive champagne!

So, it's up to you to do a good sales job on the seller so they trust you and are prepared to work with you to make both of your goals a reality. You can always remind them that without offering seller finance, their prospects of agreeing a deal at the price they want reduce substantially; not least because there's far less cash buyers about, but the availability of finance from traditional sources for 100% of the agreed purchase price of the business will be almost non-existent.

Work with them to create a win-win.

As an example, let's say you want to acquire a business and you want to negotiate payment over a few years. This 'deferred payment' essentially means you'll make an initial down payment, and then make regular payments over the course of the next several months or years depending upon the agreement you reach with the seller. This is a bit like buying a car on finance.

If the seller is trying to sell you a lemon and hope they're going to sail off into the sunset with a large suitcase full of cash, by using this method, you quickly bring an end to those pipe dreams, so don't be surprised if the deal then falls apart. However, any seller that's willing to stay on for a certain period, to help you manage and run the business over two-to-three years, is likely selling you a solid business so you can have some faith and trust in what you're buying.

If something comes out of the woodwork later that hasn't been disclosed, (or worse, concealed), you're in a far stronger position to renegotiate the overall purchase price or terms of the deal to account for these anomalies.

Making Multiple Offers

A hidden secret you won't learn anywhere else is the idea of making multiple offers on the same business. Now this is not some dodgy negotiating strategy involving a 'strawman', (a strawman is where you get a friend or family member to pose as another buyer who then makes a very low offer, so yours looks fantastic in comparison - you'll also have a good idea if the seller is telling the truth about how many offers they've received or how many people they're negotiating with – but we're not recommending you to do this, okay?).

By making one offer on a business, you put the seller in a position where it's 'take it or leave it' (remember this from Volume I?). By making multiple offers on the business where the terms vary, you put yourself in a stronger position as now the seller has a choice to decide which option works best for them (remember the Gold, Silver & Bronze fee structures we offer our clients?). Making different offers does depend on the seller's ability to grasp the options you're proposing as some won't understand or will think it's some kind of 'scam'.

If the seller has the fixed idea of receiving a large suitcase full of cash on day one and sailing off into the sunset, this is pretty much a red flag, so think about walking away from the deal. If they're unwilling to be flexible, then move onto the next deal. They may come back to you in the future once their pain is far greater.

You Name The Price, We Name The Terms

This is a secret negotiating strategy we learnt from Dan Pena (he's not for the easily offended in case you're thinking about looking him up on YouTube!).

There's a lot of moving parts you can use to get to a deal that works for both parties. If you're struggling to get the seller to agree to something, or you think they may have unrealistic price expectations, simply say to them; "I tell you what, how about we agree to this – you name the price, and I'll name the terms?"

Yes, you're potentially giving the seller the opportunity to name a huge price, but your safeguard is the terms of the deal. If a seller were to say they want £10,000,000 for a business that's only worth £2,000,000, your response could be to defer £8,000,000 for 35 years and propose a deal structure which pays them the £2,000,000 over the next 36 months. Now the seller might not agree, but the point is, it's a push-pull way of getting to a deal that works for both. Or you could agree nominal payments of say £25,000 over a long period of time with a balloon payment (lump sum), at the end of the deal.

Following Up

In our experience, depending upon a huge number of factors, you may or may not be successful in agreeing a deal quickly, and it will likely take many months, if not years to find the right business for you. This is especially true if you don't have big pots of cash to work with and you're having to structure creative deals.

You may well have to endure the frustrating experience of making offers on lots of different businesses which are all refused or don't pan out for whatever reason, but that doesn't mean the seller won't say 'yes' eventually.

Like winning instructions from potential clients, going through the process of receiving several 'no's' will put you on the pathway to receiving the one 'yes' that's best matched for you.

Bearing in mind the uncertainty in the global economy right now, with the post-pandemic impacts on supply chains across the world, and inflation starting to run out of control, a global recession (or more likely depression), could be here right now.

So, whilst it's easy to get deals done by borrowing tons of money, getting investor partners on board, and paying over the odds for a business after the recent boom, run a risk assessment on the impacts of a 20-40% reduction in turnover and profitability. If you can handle the business under these circumstances (which might involve making some very difficult decisions to ensure its survival), then you could have the deal that's right for you.

It's also worth pointing out that we're big believers in what's meant to be is meant to be, and if a deal doesn't work out, sometimes it's because there's something that you can't see right now but it will make itself apparent in the future. So don't get too disheartened – a deal not working out could save you from financial ruin (as it did for us with the law firm who had a loan shark as a partner!).

Chances Of Selling A Business

The following statistics may help you to focus the seller mind on the prospects of selling their company. They make very interesting reading:

1. The average life span of a SME (Small to Medium Size Enterprise), in the UK is 8.5 years.
2. There are 4.2 million registered companies, **yet only 10,000 sell every year.**
3. This roughly translates to only 2% of businesses selling whilst the other 98% either end up dissolving, going bust or winding up.

Essentially, you're offering a 1 in 50 chance for the seller to achieve a decent outcome in the sale of their business. In other words, the odds are grossly stacked against them to sell and realise some cash to show for their hard work. If they want to sell, they need to be reasonable with their expectations. This is why it's so important to have a follow up system with sellers to keep in contact with them if they've refused your initial offer(s) so you can see if they've managed to achieve a sale. Chances are they won't have, so it opens the door for another round of negotiations.

The Secrets Of Seller Motivation

Unless the seller's pain is great enough, there's limited motivation for them to agree a deal. They may have put the business up for sale to stroke their own ego and see what the market might pay, it may be to placate a Bank or other lender who's threatening to call in a loan, or it could be because they're going through some very pressing personal circumstances like ill-health. There's a lot of factors involved, so it's up to you to understand their situation and motivation for selling.

However, it's unlikely they will tell you their circumstance, particularly if it's an ugly situation they're in. So always ask them why they've decided to sell. Then make sure you ask them again later on and compare the answers.

An old property mentor of ours was particularly good at finding out what a seller's motivation was. He would talk to them on the phone initially and ask them why they're selling. Then when he went to visit the house, he would ask them again at the beginning of the conversation before looking around. Then he would play the 'daft old man' (his words), and say, "I'm sure you told me this before, but why are you selling?"

He would keep asking different variations of this question and comparing answers if he thought they weren't telling the truth. And the reason he did this is because if they were in a desperate situation financially, it could potentially affect his ability to buy in the first place or impact the speed at which the deal would have to go through. Both could affect the amount of time, effort, and money he would be investing initially without any guarantee of a return.

If he made an offer and the seller was going through a repossession, he could invest £1-2,000 in legal fees to move quickly, only to lose this cash if the deal didn't happen. The same thing can happen to you (multiplied by 10), when it comes to buying a business. So, establishing seller motivation is essential and if they're not motivated enough, don't invest a ton of cash in professional time to cover due diligence.

That said, if a seller is genuinely motivated, they will likely tell you their personal circumstances and work with you to finalise a deal asap.

Lock Out Agreement

Before you dip your hand in your pocket and start shelling out for a bunch of professional time with lawyers and accountants to trawl through the target acquisition's business and books, you want to protect your interests as much as possible. One thing you don't want is to spend all this cash and then see the seller turn around and sell the business to someone else!

It's common practice to agree a period of time between the buyer and seller, where they have 'exclusivity' on the deal and can complete their due diligence without the risk of the seller doing a deal elsewhere. As a buyer, you must get a lock-out agreement in place to protect yourself. This can simply be a letter of agreement between both parties where the buyer has six weeks to carry out their due diligence. You might want to test the seller and see if they will agree to cover your costs should they decide to sell it to someone else during this lock-out agreement period. If they won't, it could be a sign they're not as committed to the deal as you are.

The ideal situation is the due diligence checks out and the business is as the seller described, so you can proceed to buy it on the terms you've already agreed. But invariably, there may be things which come up and need to be addressed. The rapport you've built with the seller will determine if this is a minor blip which can be quickly overcome, or if it's a major hurdle in the road that kills the deal.

Due Diligence

An important secret to share to help conclude a deal is going through the due diligence process. This process double-checks everything the seller has told you, against the evidence which exists within the company. This may include bank statements, company accounts, management accounts, business plans, PAYE records, supplier agreements and mission, visions, and values statements.

The process of going through all this information can take a lot of time and involve a ton of cash if you're going to hire professionals to do the work. We do recommend using them as they will likely know a lot more than you do about the make-up of accounts and the cashflow position of the business, however there are secret techniques you can employ to make sure your bank account isn't being emptied into their pockets!

Not everyone's motivation in business is purely financial. Some people want to be involved with a 'mover & shaker' who's going places, and if you can provide an exciting overview of what you're trying to achieve, you'll be amazed at the talent you can attract to you, who will want to work with you for rewards that are not purely financial. This could be personal recognition, being involved with an exciting team, the realisation of a personal dream, or for equity in the proposed deal.

Sorting the wheat from the chaff of personal advisors can take a lot of time, but it's worth it to find the right people to work with. You're looking for those who don't just want to send you an invoice and expect payment the following week. You're looking for people who get inspired by your ideas and who share with you how they can help you achieve it. They'll tell you their terms but may be open to negotiation. If someone is trying to sell you on an hourly rate, this is probably not the right match for you, but if they tell you their normal rate and are willing to work on a nominal wage and equity basis, it's likely they're the right person for the job.

The Beauty Of Selling Equity

One of the things we personally love about buying and selling businesses, is the ultimate freedom and flexibility that exists, and selling equity in your firm can be a great way to achieve your goals, without diluting your shareholding too much.

You can secure some great talent on performance related earn-ins of very low percentage equity stakes (single digits), provided the deal makes sense and they can see a bright future. That's your job to sell them on a bright future of working with you as part of this company, which you should be pretty good at considering your profession and the fact you're used to selling yourself every day!

The point is, selling equity is essentially a paper exercise (meaning no money leaves your pocket), and the right people will work far harder as a 'company owner' than as an "advisor" on an hourly rate. They'll want to see the company succeed, so will go beyond the call of duty to do so, rather than coasting along and invoicing you for every little thing they do. If you need an emergency meeting, or late-night phone call, they're far more motivated to be involved than not.

Even better, selling equity in exchange for professional skills puts you in the strong position of achieving far greater value for money. The mindset is different as those parties will be more focussed on making the business work and lowering the impact on costs, so their professional time will be rewarded through a share of profits and a share of the overall sale price when you eventually decide to sell (or buy them out). Plus, if you haven't got a ton of cash in the bank, it's the easiest way to get started.

The Secret Of Iteration

Iterating means making changes, or 'pivoting' in your business. If you've ever read The Lean Start-Up or any similar books, you'll more than likely be familiar with the word.

Most of the hugely successful companies in the world have pivoted, sometimes several times, to find the right product-market fit which allowed their business to take off. The reason we raise this now is because there may be opportunities which exist in your own business, or target acquisitions, that are not being taken advantage of, because the business owners have fixed thoughts in their mind about what the business does. As such, bigger opportunities may be overlooked which could be taken advantage of, if only they iterated.

So, when you're looking at potential target acquisitions, be mindful of the fact that the business may be an unexplored goldmine if you can see angles which the current owner can't. Bear in mind, the seller will likely sell you on the fact that the business is 'going to the moon' and will talk a great game about its potential.

If that were true, we simply have to ask why the current owners haven't taken advantage of the same opportunities? They'll fumble, giving you a weak answer to this question, but that doesn't mean there's not genuine opportunities which can take advantage of.

Having gone through these books, you can apply the secrets to realise the potential in your own business, as well as any strategic or complimentary acquisitions. Whilst it's true there's very little true innovation, looking outside your industry to see the way things are being done elsewhere, and then bringing those ideas into the real estate profession can be one of the best ways to give your company a significant USP.

If you want to know how you can really add value to your clients and your business, there's a ton of extra resources we can share with you on a call.

We just ask you to invest 30 minutes into a complimentary consultation, where we can help fast-track your success (with no hard sell whatsoever).

Here's the link to book your call:

http://www.wiggywam.co.uk/estateagentssecretscall

CHAPTER TEN

THE SECRET OF THE GRAND FINALE

Despite the feeling of immortality that overshadows us in our youth, at some point, you will want to make an exit from your business empire. This can be for a variety of reasons, most of which you hope won't happen.

Ultimately, we'd all like to work hard for a bit and then retire (early) with a golden parachute as we exit our company for millions before jetting off into the sunset to slurp cocktails lying on a golden beach working on our tan...

The reality for most business owners is far from this, and that's largely because they fail to plan for their exit. They get caught up in the hum-drum day-to-day work of their business and before they know it, they're close to retirement before they even think of selling. And naturally, after a lifetime of hard work in the company, it must be worth the fortune required to fund their retirement in opulent luxury!

Most start the selling process far too late, but with optimism, by appointing a business broker who has less of a clue how to value a business than you do. They charge an up-front fee, throws a few adverts out there, and field some enquiries, all of which seem designed to frustrate as many potential buyers as possible. Then when a few hopeful buyers start digging below the surface and table offers much lower than what the broker has suggested its worth, they laugh it off and wait for that big ol' suitcase full of cash to arrive...

But the problem is, it doesn't.

And every month that passes, the seller gets older, and any personally distressing situation may become much worse. There's also a lack of motivation to keep turning up at the office as they'd rather be on the golf course now they've mentally checked out and decided it's time to sell. But the buyer hasn't arrived yet. So the company limps along with the seller having unrealistic price expectations in their mind until eventually there comes a crunch point...

The seller either decides to close the business or sell it for far less than its worth. And when they reach this point, they end up losing a ton of cash because of unrealistic expectations to begin with. If only they'd been sensible at the start...

Here's an illustrative example that's hot off the press. We were introduced to a business a few years ago and long story short, agreed to pay the seller £300,000 for it on terms. The seller wanted to sell but remain with the business for 4 years until he retired aged 70. Whilst the broad structure was agreed, the deal never got across the line as the seller got caught up in 'analysis paralysis' and slowly strangled the deal to death through months of irrelevant back-and-forth emails that took us nowhere...

Fast forward two years - there was a meeting of minds between us and the seller who now had greater pressure to sell due to his wife's illness. This increased the seller's motivation to the point where he was prepared to work reduced hours in the business and would sell it for £100,000.

Now, he's already "lost" £200,000 in value due to procrastination and not getting the original deal done.

Then it comes to light that he still isn't making a decision now either because he's allowing a business advisor (with ulterior motives and who isn't acting in the seller's best interests), and a secretary to call the shots!

Bang!

Another five-page email asking the most ridiculous hypothetical questions you've ever heard and running a million different 'what-if' scenario's that are so far removed from reality as to be untrue. Oh, and that's after he disappeared on holiday when the draft heads of terms paperwork was being drawn up and didn't tell anyone where he was going...

These are the sorts of scenario's people put themselves in. So, what now?

Well, for us, the fact that a seller behaves so irrationally ultimately kills the deal. Not only has he recently lost a fortune on his pension because of inaction, but he's also lost a fortune in the value of his business and it's now become a millstone around his neck which no-one else can buy.

So, he either closes the business (which will cost him c.£250,000), or he'll quite literally 'die in the saddle' of old age and it will be left to his wife and children to sort out. Not exactly a win-win, but entirely of his own making.

How could this scenario be different?

Well, let's look at what could have happened if he'd planned to exit the business early. In doing so, he could have put the following in place:

1) **A 'junior' management board** – transferring responsibility for running the firm to a junior management board would help tremendously by removing a lot of the burdens from the business owner's shoulders. It also means the direction of the firm is not dependant on one person, and can be run, with standard operating procedures, a mission, a vision, a set of values and goals.

2) **Standard Operating Procedures (SOP's)** – building out a file full of SOP's means all staff know exactly how things should be done, and again, removes the need for them to put all the problems on the boss's desk. A SOP should be a structure which empowers the staff, rather than dictates to them.

3) **Mission, Vision & Values (MVV's)** – this is fundamental to inspire and motivate staff towards a bright future for the company and encourage them to take ownership of their individual roles by becoming solution-orientated, rather than 'problem-elevation' orientated (passing all problems to the boss!).

4) **Monthly Management Accounts (MMA's)** – these are vital to keep the finger on the pulse of the business to ensure its functioning as it should. They also give great insight and transparency into the numbers so all the staff have visibility on what needs to happen to cover the overheads. It also makes it very easy for any potential buyer to assess the true value of the company, especially if you've had MMA's in place for the last 3 years.

5) **Transparent Accounts** – this causes some upset with business owners who don't like paying tax, so they do all sorts of 'hooky'

things within their business to try and reduce the profits, so they pay less tax. The problem is, once they come to sell, the business appears only marginally profitable, so any buyer will base their decision strictly on the set of numbers they have in front of them. The seller will then try and talk a great game and say how profitable the business really is, but you won't be able to find any evidence of that, so don't be tempted to pay more on the hope that there's hidden profits that you can harvest at a later date. (The worst example we saw was in LA when we looked at an auto-repair business. The owners had <u>zero</u> financials to show us but told us it was making some serious cash. We had no information to verify their comments, and simply said we'd be prepared to buy the business, but it would have to be on an open-book profit share over the next 3 years. The seller replied that he could show us a pallet full of cash to prove how profitable the business was (think Breaking Bad…). Needless to say, we couldn't agree a deal!).

6) **Copies of the last three years bank statements in PDF and Excel format** – this proves the business has nothing to hide and is being completely open about its financial position. The PDF records each transaction, whilst the spreadsheet allows rapid changing of a number of variables for any buyer to assess the impact the changes they make will have on the business and saves them a ton of work in due diligence. This especially helps if they don't have MMA's and you want to build up some draft ones to work with.

7) **Watertight contracts of employment with staff** – having all staff on a standard contract with notice periods in place will give reassurance that the business is being run properly.

8) **Online data room** – simply a place where you store all these digital documents which a potential buyer can access and review. Putting it together saves you a ton of time sending documents to different parties and shows you're being transparent in the process.

9) **Business and marketing plan** – a helpful document to show where the business is heading and how it's currently generating work from as well as any other marketing channels that may be open to the company.

10) **A fair sales figure in mind & the offer of seller-finance** – if a seller is reasonable in their expectations, and they've put all the above

in place, it makes the sales process far easier. The conversation is more transparent and gives the buyer more peace of mind that they're not walking into a bear trap. Offering seller finance is the clincher that so many brokers don't do, simply because most get paid a percentage of the cash that changes hands between both parties. Putting it on the table for the buyer makes closing the deal easier but use some mechanism where you're getting regular financial updates on business performance and where you can intervene if the business looks like its performance is suffering.

One secret to consider given to us by a business mentor, is to make plans to sell a business **as soon as you acquire it**. His pet phrase was, "the best time to sell a business is now" because it did away with any possible complications in the market or wider economy which could change at a moment's notice and wipe out the business.

Whilst businesses can be good income providers, taking a business and flipping it for a profit can be great for building your wealth quickly. Plus, you have none of the headaches involved in running the firm, so you have more control over your time which you can now spend looking for the next deal.

This may or may not appeal depending upon your age, ambition, and motivation, but it's worth considering whether or not to spend the next three years rapidly expanding your business via mergers and acquisitions, before selling it to a bigger company and retiring with a big cash lump sum that would take years to generate in cashflow.

As always, the decision is yours, and we're here to help you as much as we possibly can.

If you've been following what we're saying here and started implementing the plan to exit your business early, you should find yourself in the position where you can effectively make yourself redundant. This is important for several reasons, the least of all is it helps you to massively build your wealth – a promise we made to you right at the start of our journey together.

Come again? How exactly does making myself redundant build my wealth…?

Well think about it this way – which is more valuable:

Business A) The owner regularly works 60-80 hours a week, all the problems end up on his desk and the business is marginally profitable. He hasn't had a holiday in 3 years because his last holiday abroad was constantly interrupted with telephone calls and emails from staff who couldn't handle the simplest of issues which needed to be resolved.

Business B) The owner works around 2 hours a week checking in with the management board and reviewing the financial statements to ensure the business is hitting target. She has her finger on the pulse observing market trends and annual changes in the business as well as reviewing the wider economy, so she's able to act quickly with her team and implement changes when they need to happen. The business is hugely profitable and anyone looking to take over could read and understand the standard operating procedures within 5-6 hours.

It doesn't take a genius to figure out that business B is worth significantly more. How much more? Would you pay 2-3 times more? How about 4-5?

Obviously, you would look at all the numbers before making a snap judgment, but the simple point is, Business A has very little value unless someone knows how to turn Business A into Business B. Even then, due to the significant amount of work involved, you wouldn't want to pay over the odds for the first business. In many cases, such businesses are sold for £1.00, or they're forced to close their doors when the owner finally gives up because they've had enough which position do you want to be in?

So, you can see why we've taken the time to take you through this intensive process over these three Volumes – by doing so, you've taken your business from unsaleable and a source of stress, to something that's actively building your wealth, making you more profitable and which you should be able to sell for around three times profitability and retire early to live the life of your dreams.

But nothing happens without action in applying all that you've learnt in these three volumes.

So, if you're ready to take action on what you've already learnt and want to fast-track your success, this is your final opportunity to take advantage of our free 30-minute consultation call before you close the book on this opportunity forever.

We'll show you how to add value to your clients and your business, plus there's a ton of extra resources we can share with you on a call.

We just ask you to take it seriously and invest 30 minutes into the consultation, where we can help fast-track your success.

Here's the link to book your call:

http://www.wiggywam.co.uk/estateagentssecretscall

CONCLUSION

Congratulations on making it to the end of Volume III.

The only thing standing between you making a dramatic difference to your business by applying all you've learnt so far, is your ability to execute on your new-found knowledge.

So many people enjoy reading a book, learn some new things which they can impress their friends with, and then close the book without ever applying those things to their life or business. We don't want you to be one of them.

If you're finding it difficult to implement what you've learnt, having some accountability from an independent third party can be the one thing you need to fast-track your success.

We offer an exclusive 12-week training program, dedicated to handholding you through the transformation of your business by implementing this roadmap, to get the results you deserve.

If you'd like to know more, the first step is to book in a complimentary 30-minute consultation, so we can find out more about your goals and dreams, and how we can help you get there as quickly as possible.

Here's the link to book the call:

http://www.wiggywam.co.uk/estateagentssecretscall

ABOUT THE AUTHOR

Silas is the author of a number of property related books including the Estate Agent's Secrets Trilogy, and As Safe As Houses – Cracking The Code To Profitable Property Investment. He also explores the more spiritual side of life in his book – Love Is The New Religion.

As someone who has been in property all his life, he's passionate about using his decades of experience to improve the home buying, selling, and renting journey, to help everyone involved.

Despite working in the family business from the age of 9, Silas's first real job was as an estate agent, and he fell in love with the industry at 18. He then trained to become a Building Surveyor to understand property at a deeper level, before going on to become a property investor in 2007, buying his first buy-to-let property about 5 minutes before the credit crunch recession gripped the UK!

Despite these setbacks and challenges, he went on to build a respectable property portfolio before training others how to replicate his success working alongside such household names as Martin Roberts from Homes Under The Hammer, Robbie Fowler (the footballer), and internationally renowned author Robert Kiyosaki.

Frustrated at the length of time it takes to buy and sell for most people and having bought and sold homes in days as an investor, Silas turned his attention to doing something about changing the way the UK housing market works.

This led him to start WiggyWam – the UK's first property platform built as a collaborative communication bridge between estate agents and lawyers, to get deals done far more quickly.

WiggyWam's mission is to remove the barriers people face when moving home and the company is constantly on the lookout for collaborative opportunities to work with likeminded individuals and companies who share the same mission and values. You can find out more at
www.wiggywam.co.uk

Printed in Great Britain
by Amazon

21030054R00095